THE Mum WHO ROARED

A COMPLETE A–Z GUIDE TO

loving your mind, body and attitude

AFTER BABY

CHRISTIE NICHOLAS

EXISLE
PUBLISHING

First published 2011

Exisle Publishing Limited
'Moonrising', Narone Creek Road, Wollombi,
NSW 2325, Australia
P.O. Box 60–490, Titirangi, Auckland 0642,
New Zealand
www.exislepublishing.com

National Library of Australia Cataloguing-in-
Publication Data:

Nicholas, Christie

The mum who roared : a complete a–z guide to
loving your mind, body and attitude after baby /
Christie Nicholas.

ISBN 9781921497889 (pbk.)

Includes index.

Mothers—Life skills guides.
Motherhood.

646.70082

Designed by Tracey Gibbs
Illustrations by Tracey Gibbs
Typeset in Calibri, Bebas and Metro Script
Printed in Singapore by KHL Printing Co Pte Ltd

This book uses paper sourced under ISO 14001
guidelines from well-managed forests and other
controlled sources.

10 9 8 7 6 5 4 3 2 1

Disclaimer

Before you begin any diet, exercise or treatment program, consult a qualified health practitioner. Everyone has different needs and therefore your needs may affect the suitability of the suggestions and recommendations stipulated in this book. Content in this book should not replace the advice provided by health practitioners. Neither the author nor the publisher and their distributors can be held responsible for any loss, claim or action that may arise from reliance on the information contained in this book.

CONTENTS

♡♡♡

This book is dedicated to the two girls who inspire my life and to the husband who made this possible.

INTRODUCTION

What this book is about and why you'll want to read it

Since becoming a mum, have you ever woken up and not recognised who you are any more? Are you unclear of what you want from your life or have you lost sight of your goals? Have you neglected yourself and everything that once made you *you*? Or maybe you are just overwhelmed by the pressure and expectations that come with motherhood and are desperate for some motivation so you can actually enjoy being a woman who also happens to be a mum.

Whether you have just become a mother for the first time or are an old timer feeling lost and unmotivated, you are sharing similar experiences. From time to time all mums find themselves drained emotionally, physically and personally from having a new baby, new identity and new life to adjust to. Whether we have just given birth or are sending our children to high school, there are many moments when we all find ourselves thinking, 'When am I going to figure this all out?', 'How can I feel good about myself again?' and, my favourite, 'Is this it?'

The role of mum can be so intense that you soon forget you are also an individual. You get so absorbed by the demands of motherhood that it's easy to start losing your X-factor and the key ingredients that made you the woman you are. Without recognising the warning signs, you slip into a mundane routine and just focus on the daily activities that come with being a mum and forget, or make excuses for forgetting, everything else.

Slowly, you start to neglect your role as a passionate woman who once had dreams, aspirations, sex appeal, other interests and a zest for life. How many times have you found yourself saying, 'I don't have time', 'I don't have the energy', 'There are too many other things to do', 'When the kids are older' or 'I just can't be bothered'?

And it's all too easy to do this. Let's face it: motherhood is overwhelming. It is even more overwhelming when you are a new mum or an existing mum with zero support to get you through the difficult periods. Not all of us realised what we were signing up for and not all of us have someone to tell us how we can be a mum and a woman at the same time and actually get through it all relatively unscathed.

The Mum Who Roared is your starting point to having a greater love and respect for your mind, body and attitude. In it, mums from all backgrounds, nationalities, economic statuses, with children young and older, share the key tactics they implemented to feel happier, more motivated, passionate, fulfilled and balanced. After all, no one needs to tell us how hard it is to be a mother in this day and age, but they can tell us what we can do to make the role easier.

Importantly, this book is a friendly, real and practical guide to adjusting to your role as a mum. It is not a parenting guide. Instead, this motivating resource provides simple and effective tips so that you can genuinely enjoy this next chapter in your life, feel in control and stay in touch with your core needs and values.

Whether you are a new mum or simply a mum looking for some motivation, this book provides ideas that can be implemented into real lifestyles immediately and that are relevant for life, not just the early days of motherhood — ideas that will make life easier and make you feel better mentally, physically and personally. *The Mum Who*

Roared tackles ways to take care of *you* during this daunting, exhilarating and demanding phase. It recognises that you are a woman, not just a mum. So by following some of the suggestions, reading other real-life accounts and survival tips, and using the practical pull-out goal cards, you can continue your journey as a happy, healthy, balanced woman, who is also a mum ... A mum who roared!

Visit
www.themumwhoroared.com for
more inspiration and motivation!

CHAPTER 1

My story

Like most new mums, I was blown away with how dramatically my life changed when the baby came along. It wasn't just the nappies, messy household, permanent muffin-top, saggy boobs and boring routine that got to me. These were just the tip of the iceberg. I had a hard time adjusting to a whole list of things.

I thought that when I became a mum I would enjoy my year off work to be with my baby, have a wonderful time meeting other mums for coffee, have a perfectly clean home, dinner on the table at 6 p.m. and be ready to continue with my career at the end of maternity leave *if* I felt like it — because I was sure I would have the choice. (I hadn't yet realised that without a mortgage fairy or a husband willing to take a second job, there really isn't a choice.) This was pretty much the extent of my vision of motherhood and my new role. You'd be forgiven for thinking this all sounds very, very reasonable (on paper anyway).

But there were so many things nobody told me! For starters, your brain doesn't quite work the same way any more. Now it always has something you are totally responsible for influencing your every move and decision and naturally taking precedence over everything, including when you eat, sleep or go to the toilet. This was new. Now everything I did had a direct consequence on a human life, a life dependent on me.

I remember telling my mum when I was fresh out of hospital, 'Mum, my head hurts because I am always thinking about her [the baby]. I just can't switch off and relax a little. When does my brain start to feel like normal again?' She told me to wait another 21 years and it would start to get a little easier. I honestly thought that this switch in gears in my mind was temporary and that I would feel like myself again in a few days. But it's just not like that. You have to get to know and accept a new version of yourself.

Right from the beginning, I found myself naturally sacrificing my needs. It was anything from foregoing a new bra or outfit for me to pay for nice things for her to putting further studies and my career on hold because I felt it was more important to be there for the baby. At the time I didn't mind giving these things up because, like most parents, I would do anything for my child if I believed it was for the best, but I did have to quickly review what I *was* doing for myself and how I *was* actually going to address my needs, all while giving my child everything I possibly could in terms of time, love and material things. This became a juggling act and, at times, a stressful one.

I didn't realise that losing an income when I went on maternity leave would bother me so much. But it did. Even though I chose not to work for a variety of reasons, realistically, without the extra income you just can't buy and do what you are used to. We weren't going to live on the streets any time soon, but spending habits did have to change dramatically. I had to get used to living without those nice things that made me feel all warm and fuzzy as well as holidays and outings, and accept having a little less financial freedom. What do people do without retail therapy? (They call it that for a reason, after all!) I had to find other activities to satisfy my superficial reliance on these splurges.

To make the situation even harder, when I stopped working to go on maternity leave, my sense of value and self-worth started to disappear. In my corporate life I would get acknowledged for good work, receive a bonus for my efforts and even a promotion when I stepped up to the plate. Now, nobody said thanks to me for getting up at 4 a.m., having dinner ready on time, juggling all the domestic duties, or for going to the effort of puréeing apple instead of opening a ready-to-eat jar. I started to feel unappreciated and worthless and my identity was challenged and obscured. Sadly, I even found myself telling my husband what I had cleaned that day so I could justify the importance of my contribution and get a thankyou.

What had happened to the woman who managed million-dollar budgets, negotiated contracts and spoke to a packed auditorium? I realised that my corporate role and the duties that came with it had shaped my identity. Without the work meetings, responsibilities, emails and professional achievements and accolades, I didn't know who I was any more or what else to take pride in. Unfortunately, I had allowed my job to influence who I was, and without it, I felt I was nothing. How was I going to become someone again or, more frighteningly, *who* was I going to become?

In the beginning of motherhood I was bored with myself and my personality in general and figured everyone else would be as well. Other than my life as mum, I didn't know what else I could even talk about now. I didn't have any other interests or passions.

Then there was my image. My body did not bounce back after having the baby, my hair did fall out after my first haircut after giving birth (so I looked slightly bald), and one boob was bigger than the other thanks to breastfeeding. I was amazed at the similarities my belly had to a fresh ball of (family-size) pizza dough — very soft, spongy, white and dimply all over. As a result, I had no idea how to dress myself any more now that I didn't have to rely on maternity clothes. I felt frumpy, and this a sexy woman did not make. But how was I going to get back some va-va-voom? I was a mum after all. Could mums, or should mums, even look sexy? Were my days of push-up bras, killer heels and sexy dresses behind me? Was a XXX-Brazilian now out of the question? And when, oh when, would a fat, sweaty workman with an exposed butt crack ever give me a wolf-whistle again? Aaah, those were the days ...

Unfortunately, my husband was working seven days a week in a family business and none of my close friends had babies, so I didn't have someone to hold my hand, relieve me for a little while or tell me what to do to get through the miserable days — and there were many. Sometimes I walked the streets with the pram for hours, bawling my eyes out. Other days I stayed in my PJs until 4 p.m. and just got by, hour by hour. I shudder at the thought of those days and the heavy, heavy feeling that weighed down my whole mind and body (and that feeling wasn't just coming from the 10 kilos I had yet to lose). It wasn't even depression. I was just thrown by my new responsibilities, new life and uncertain outlook for myself and my future. Like all mums, I was in the process of figuring it all out.

And I will admit, shock horror, that the stay-at-home routine bored me some days and wore me out on others. I mean, how many times in a week can you go to the park? How many times in the day can you sing 'Twinkle Twinkle Little Star'? Who really wants a Wiggles song stuck in their head all day and does anybody *really* enjoy housework? I know I don't. In fact, I prefer not to do it at all. But I was trapped because I knew that this was my life, for now. I committed to being home with my child, for the first year anyway, and to do what was traditionally expected of a stay-at-home mum. Even though I gave 110 per cent to my baby, I guess it is safe to say that a few things were getting to me along the way.

I could go on and on about my experiences as a new mum, but the point is that I found myself all over the place, questioning who I was, resentful of my situation and wondering how and if I was going to feel passionate about anything else again, other than my beautiful baby (who was, by the way, everything I wanted and more). I felt so extraordinarily ordinary and that just wasn't enough for me.

As women in the 21st century, we have grown up being told we can have it all, to aim high and that we are capable of everything. I believed all this. So it was a rude awakening when I found I couldn't and didn't have it all, that there wasn't enough time, energy or resources to reach for the sky, and that I was unable to do everything

I wanted to do. My bubble had burst because my expectations of myself did not match real life. I didn't know whether to want what I had or find a way to have what I wanted. Did everyone feel like this?

My issue wasn't simply adjusting to having a baby in the house. It was finding out how I was going to feel like the vibrant woman I wanted to be while being a mum and tackling head on all the issues mums face day to day. I wanted so desperately to be a great woman and a mum who roared at the same time. I wanted to have things other than a baby to talk about. I needed something to put the fire back in my belly, a little X-factor, and to be genuinely happy that my life and I were in order.

✳✳✳

About six months into my journey it all clicked. I was happy. I had my body back. I had a passion that made my mind tick. I loved myself again, what I was doing and where I was going. I had had an interesting journey of self-discovery while being completely overwhelmed by the extreme ups and downs of typical motherhood, yet I felt great about my role, what I had achieved and my future. Why was I feeling like this? The answer was simple. I had a happy, healthy, balanced life and attitude that kept me positive. I had made changes to improve myself personally, physically and mentally.

It wasn't long afterwards that my best friend had a baby. She was at the beginning of the journey I had just finished, crying and saying everything I had felt when I started. She felt overwhelmed, incapable, isolated, tired and as if she was sinking into a pit of misery. She was just getting by, doing what a mother had to do, in between hormonal breakdowns and feelings of uncertainty, hoping and praying for a better day. I thought about everything she said and how similar it was to my story (and yours, I suspect) and decided to list for her every little step I took to become a better version of who I was. This was her reply:

'Hon, thanks so much for this. You couldn't have made things clearer. As soon as I read it I felt instantly better. Everything I am going through makes so much more sense. I am going to read these points daily to remind myself that I can make things better and that every bad day is followed by a good day. Now, time to get out of the pyjamas, go put on my favourite perfume and turn the music up. I'm back.'

Having seen the tips work for me and for her, I thought I would prepare them for you. I hope that this book becomes for you that friend who has been through it all before and is here to hold your hand and remind you that you are a capable, smart, desirable woman, great mum and so much more. Even if you only take away ten tips, you will have made ten positive moves to a better you.

Best of luck with your journey and I hope you become the woman you want to be as well as a mum who roared.

CHAPTER 2

What it takes to be a real yummy mummy of the 21st century

After I got through my little post-baby life crisis and started to make sense of motherhood, I was in a fairly happy place. I had figured out what made my mind tick, had a greater level of body confidence and, overall, knew I was walking around with a more positive and healthy attitude to life, living and new beginnings. I actually felt like a yummy mummy.

I didn't look like a supermodel, but I felt like one and that was why I deserved to be called a yummy mummy. My definition of a yummy mummy extended beyond the physical. As far as I was concerned, a yummy mummy had the whole package; she looked good, felt great about herself as a person and radiated a special energy.

I conducted a survey to see what other mums thought defined a yummy mummy. Participants ranged from working mums, stay-at-home mums, single mums, mums with one child as well as those with multiple children, image-conscious mums and mums who couldn't care less about their appearance. I wanted to know how these mums defined a yummy mummy, if they viewed themselves as one, knew someone who was one, and how they thought you could become one.

The results were interesting. A yummy mummy is no longer a term used only to describe celebrity mums who look more like runway models than sleep-deprived schoolyard frumps. That celebrity mum is not someone they relate to, aspire to be or envision looking or living like. Instead, the majority of mums believe there is more to a yummy mummy than external beauty. A yummy mummy, as far as modern-day mums are concerned, is a mum who takes pride in her appearance, dedicates some time to nurturing herself, is healthy, generally positive, has outside interests and relationships, and displays a bit of spunk.

My panel of mums also gave me their tips for mothers who want to be this kind of woman and the following pages include their recommendations. But before we get to that complete A–Z guide to loving your mind, body and attitude after baby, here's a summary of the characteristics of a *real* yummy mummy of the 21st century, as defined by mums who have been there, done that, laughed, cried and survived to share their story!

Physically — a yummy mummy:

- has a healthy weight
- exercises
- maintains a routine resembling pre-baby times (such as showering daily!)
- gets out of her pyjamas before noon
- respects her body.

Emotionally — a yummy mummy:

- has the occasional cry, but not all the time
- is motivated
- has a positive perspective
- maintains relationships with those close to her
- asks for help in times of need.

Personally — a yummy mummy:

- feels pretty good about herself overall
- has outside interests
- is having fun
- maintains some sort of balance in life
- recognises her needs matter too.

CHAPTER 3

A

... is for 'Asking for help'

'Please listen carefully ladies. In the beginning everyone will offer to help you. Friends and family will clamour over each other to cook, clean, shop, babysit and relieve you in any way you please. But don't be fooled. And do not take these offers of help for granted. These offers of help will dry up after about six weeks, because by that stage everyone will believe you when you politely say you're "fine" and "everything is under control".

Take it from someone who learnt the hard way. Say "yes" to anyone who offers to help. If someone asks, "Do you want me to drop in with some dinner?" you say, "What time suits you?" If someone says, "I've got a spare afternoon this week, would you like some help with the housework?" you say, "Friday's perfect." If someone says, "Do you want me to mind the baby for a few hours so you can sleep/go out/get a massage?" you say, "Three hours would be a life-saver."

I didn't accept anywhere near enough help the first time round, but when Leo was born I didn't muck about. One of the best things I did was telling any close family who wanted to pop by for a visit to bring us a meal. This saved me shopping time and cooking time and meant there was one less thing to worry about. Not only that, I found that family actually wanted to help and felt good about contributing. So it was no skin off their noses but went a long way for me. All I can say is let go of your pride ladies and lap it up because it sure doesn't last!'

— Joni (31), mum to Ava (two) and Leo (four months)

All new mums should accept offers of help and ask for help when they need it. There is no room for pride during this time. You are tired, there are new demands in your life that you are responsible for, and chances are you don't know exactly what you are doing. On top of all this, your emotions are turbulent. As a result, in the beginning everything takes longer and feels so much harder than it really is.

Allow yourself at least six weeks to three months of extra (guilt-free) help. Not only is this when you are most likely to need it, but this is also when the kind offers from friends and family are in full swing. After this time, they expect you to have the hang of things and might not be as forthcoming with offers of assistance. So milk it while you can and use this time to rest, save your energy and enjoy the extra set of hands that will make your day that bit easier.

In the early days you might be overprotective of your baby. You might feel uncomfortable relinquishing any responsibility for caring for your child, or fear that no one knows your child the way you do. Perhaps you think you are the only one who can attend to his or her needs properly and expertly. If you think this way then you are only making things more difficult for yourself. Even if it is a case of 'mum knows best', does it really matter that much in the long run if someone else has a go for a few hours a week?

A little help from others, such as a partner or grandparents, is healthy for all. You get a break, you learn different ways to take care of the baby and you give other family members a chance to bond with the baby too.

It doesn't have to be much help to make a real difference to your day. People can help by changing a few nappies, bottle-feeding, settling, burping and bathing. All these things take time, so relinquishing even one baby responsibility a day means you will have a chance to take a bath, make a phone call or lie down for a few minutes to recharge. A small dose of help will help you feel more energised for the next shift.

You might be in charge of running the household now that you are the homemaker (I prefer the term 'domestic goddess'), and feel that you have to be totally responsible for all the jobs in the house and that you must also take care of the needs of everyone else in the family. Well, guess what? You can't — not in the beginning at least. And if you do, something else will suffer.

In the beginning, you have to let a few things go. Don't torture yourself by trying to do it all on your own because you think you have to. You can't be a supermum when you haven't yet finished reading the manual! Motherhood and adjusting to it will take time. And it's early days still. It is more important for you to catch up on sleep than it is to hang out or bring in the washing.

Accepting some help will ease you into your new routine. There is a lot involved with running a household. There are errands to attend to, shopping to do, the housework, cooking, not to mention taking care of a new baby! Don't be embarrassed asking for extra help around the home at this time. It should be expected, now more than ever.

'My mistake was never asking anyone to help me. I felt that other people had their own pressures to deal with, they didn't need mine. I also felt that I should be able to get it together on my own. But one day I just lost it. I had unexpected visitors in 45 minutes, my hubby was working, I was still in my pyjamas, the clothes washing was overflowing, there was no food in the house, the kitchen was a pigsty and my baby was due for a feed in 30 minutes, which meant I would be breastfeeding when the visitors were going to come by, and my house was upside down. I started freaking out. It all just seemed so hard. I didn't know how to even start. I was stressed, anxious and overwhelmed.

I called my mum and cried. She came over to calm me down and get the house in order. I shouldn't have let myself get to the stage where I was distressed in the first instance. I should have already had arrangements in place that every few days someone was going to pop in to help for 30 minutes. When you are taking care of a baby, what once took 30 minutes now takes three hours, so if you have two 30-minute visits from someone dedicated to taking the load off, you save yourself six hours of work. That is six hours of catch-up sleep, people!'

— Mary-Anne (34), mum to Jacob (six) and Emily (four)

Several mums I have spoken to say how much it meant to them to have someone bring over a home-cooked meal. They just asked (or told — depending on the kind of relationship they had!) a few relatives (parents and in-laws are good for this) to be on dinner duty when they come round to see the little one. They don't have to cook a three-course meal. They could even pop in with takeaway or leftovers, just as long as they brought something. Alternatively, if you know someone is coming over, ask them to stop by the supermarket on the way to pick up a few necessities you haven't had a chance to organise yourself. As you would know by now, a trip to the supermarket isn't what it used to be!

'I remember opening the door and seeing my mum holding a big casserole of food. It made me so happy I wanted to cry. Preparing a nutritious meal after a long, sometimes really difficult day was the last thing I had energy for. This was one of my highlights and something I wish for all mums.'

— Tina (38), mum to Terri (thirteen)

You might be going a little insane at times and feel like you are cooped up in the house around the clock. If you need a little time out, and you will, ask someone around to mind the baby. Take twenty minutes to walk to your local coffee shop for a latte and a chance to read the paper. If you want to feel even more comfortable, go during the baby's sleep time and bring your mobile.

There will be times when you just need to get away. This doesn't mean you are a bad mum or neglecting your child. You just need to refresh your brain to function better. Once you are comfortable with going out briefly, start extending your 'break'. You might even be able to go to the supermarket or, even better, get your hair cut!

It's likely that those who live close by, love you and want to support you would be delighted to help out with dinner, washing, cleaning and minding the baby. But they might not offer all the time in case they offend you by making you feel they think you can't do it all. It might be up to you to open up and ask for help. If you would feel guilty resting while they helped, do something together. You'll still get the place cleaned and organised, just in half the time!

You might be in the difficult position where your partner works a lot and you don't have close family or friends who live near you or are physically able to help. This can be very hard. However, even if they can't physically help, partners, friends and family can listen to you and this is also valuable. So when it feels like it's all getting a bit much, make a phone call and pour out your heart to someone. You might find that they too have been through what you are going through or worse. And while they might not be able to fix your problem, it can be soothing to know that others have gone through similar situations and come out okay.

The key point here is that you ask for help, whether that's physical, practical help or simply comfort from someone at the end of a phone.

CHAPTER 4

... is for 'Babymoon period'

Many mums feel great pressure to get on with life too soon after giving birth. Just as many feel concerned or guilt-ridden that they are letting people down if they don't continue working through their daily lives at the same pace as pre-birth. Yet our bodies have just gone through a major upheaval (and sometimes major surgery) and need a minimum of six weeks to recover, as doctors advise us.

After giving birth, resolve to give yourself some 'babymoon' time. This is basically some grace time for you to get used to having a new person in the house and also recover from the birth itself. Use this time to rest whenever possible, get through the gruelling visitors' period and recover from stitches and other uncomfortable physical symptoms. It is also vitally important to use this time to bond and get to know your baby without other un-necessary pressures, such as the pressure to cook, clean, run errands, exercise and so on.

Over the coming days and weeks you are going to be challenged mentally, physically and emotionally, and you need to prepare yourself for this. Expecting to bounce back after birth isn't fair to the baby or to you. Mums need to prioritise their needs and accept that this is one of the most important things you can do as a mother. Just take time to be with the baby and to rest. If you make an effort to consider your needs in these early weeks you will be a healthier, happier mum.

There are many cultures that value this babymoon period so much that they even have a 40-day stay-at-home tradition for new mothers. During this time, women are encouraged to stay at home purely to recover and bond with their baby. This is as much for the mother's wellbeing as it is for the child's. When you give yourself this time, you gain the headspace and energy to embrace the next phase with more confidence and peace.

'I remember going to the supermarket ten days after giving birth. It was my first time out of the house and the first time away from my baby. There was no food in the house and I wanted to get out for a little. What I thought would be a nice 30 minutes to clear my head turned out to be a really stressful excursion.

I unfortunately chose a day and time when the supermarket was busy and the checkout line I was in would not move at all. Already I was starting to feel a little overwhelmed at being in such a busy, loud environment, so far away from my quiet home.

With my trolley full and waiting earnestly to be served, my phone rang with my frantic husband shouting at me that the baby had woken up early and was crying hysterically for a feed. I started to freak out and, as a result of the stress, my boobs started madly leaking milk. I politely asked the checkout lady if she could please go a little faster because my baby needed me, but she looked at me like I had asked her for a star in the sky.

I couldn't get out of there fast enough to get home to a stressed-out hubby and baby. Not exactly the pleasant trip I thought it would be. From then on I would give my hubby mini lists so that he could just bring back the essentials and I did not leave the house again until six weeks. I just couldn't handle it.'

— Julianne (28), mum to Rubi (eighteen months)

Listen to what your body is telling you and follow your own instincts. If you want to stay in your pyjamas for the first two weeks, then do it. Give yourself permission to just switch off from the community temporarily. It is during the early weeks that we feel most emotional and sensitive, so when you enter an environment like a shopping centre or other busy environment, you can easily feel anxious and uncomfortable.

'For me, six weeks went by without blinking. I couldn't believe I hadn't left the house. I just felt like I needed to be home, resting and spending time getting to know Jamie. I just didn't have the confidence or the motivation to get out earlier. When I did actually get out, I still took baby steps. I made an effort to clean myself up, put on some lippie and a nice skirt. Mind you, I was just going down the road for a coffee, but I wanted to adjust to society slowly. It sounds weird in hindsight, but it was my first child and I didn't know what I was doing, nor did I have anyone to help me. So I just listened to my instincts and took it very slowly. That way I didn't stress out and felt more confident with myself, the baby and my abilities as each day went by.'

— Marissa (32), mum to Jamie (five) and Zara (two)

If you give yourself this time to rest in the beginning, it makes sense that you will recover more fully and have a little extra mental and physical energy. So when you do finally go out into these environments you can be more confident. After your babymoon period you will feel a little more together and ready to tackle new things. So for now relax.

Some things you can do to embrace the babymoon period

- Take the phone off the hook.
- Stay in your sleepwear for as long as you feel is necessary.
- Put up a do-not-disturb sign on the front door when you don't want interruptions.
- Outsource shopping.
- Cook meals in bulk in advance and freeze portions, ready for use.
- Stock up on non-perishables like canned foods and toiletries to avoid shopping trips.
- Break the isolation by inviting close friends or family round for a coffee.
- Request some help from close friends and family for things like a meal, laundry, errands, baby needs.

CHAPTER 5

... is for 'Confidence building'

'I always felt that my little one could sense my mood. So I thought that if she was thinking that I didn't have a clue, then she wouldn't trust me. So I always acted like I knew what I was doing, until I figured out what I was supposed to be doing! I wanted her to trust me. When I could see that she did, she was calm and content and as a result I felt reassured that I was on the right track. I say fake it 'til you make it.'

— Marnie (36), mum to Casey (four)

Even if you have done all the reading in the world and been around babies since forever, you will have moments when you feel your confidence being tested. Don't give up on yourself. Just practise what you have learnt, follow your gut and ask for help. Trust the knowledge that you do have and allow yourself some time to figure out the rest. It will take some time to get to know how your new bundle of joy operates and the best way to handle settling, feeding, sleep deprivation and a constantly changing routine.

A key ingredient to being a great mum is having self-confidence and the genuine belief that you are more than capable. Your new baby, routine and hormones will test your confidence just when you need it most. But, rest assured, the more confident you become, the less stressed you will feel and the more likely it is you will continue to manage and flourish in your role. As a result, your child will also be calmer, things will continue to run smoothly in the home and you will cope better in unpredictable environments outside the home.

'I finally mustered the confidence to put the baby in the pram and go to the local café for a much needed coffee. Out of the blue, my newborn started crying hysterically for a feed. I was halfway between the house and the café and anyone with a newborn crying out for food knows how painful it sounds. For a second I just panicked. Do I start running back to safety? There wasn't anyone there who could tell me what to do. And there was no time to race back home or to the café so I just sat on a stranger's fence and popped the boob out.

Other than a car driving by with some louts, I survived it. As a result, I calmed down, baby calmed down and we could continue to the café. If I'd let myself panic and run back home, I doubt very much I would have gone out again. But I just made the best of the situation and prioritised the need to stay calm and in control. Baby followed suit and I had more confidence for next time, knowing I could actually manage a stressed-out baby in public and survive to tell the story. Mission accomplished.'

— Janine (27), mum to Andrew (nine months)

Regardless of your preparation, expectations and level of support for this new, scary period in your life, your confidence can be affected by all the changes, many of which you would never have experienced before. Sometimes the factors that affect your confidence are for reasons beyond your control, but by recognising them you can learn how to better manage your feelings.

1. Physical changes — our bodies have just gone through something extraordinary and our hormones are all over the place. We are also seriously sleep deprived and as a result quite sensitive. All this makes us feel as if everything is so much worse than it really is.

2. Emotional pressure — a baby can bring with it more pressure and work for you than you expected or prepared for. The baby will also change the dynamics of the household and your relationship with your partner and family. Things are never going to be the same again and this takes time to get used to.

3. Economic changes — if you have dropped an income it will affect your independence and freedom to live the way in which you were accustomed. It will take some adjusting to feel confident and happy while sacrificing some material things you used to value.

4. Society's expectations — a new mum will feel pressure to live up to society's expectations of what a mum should be. Confidence will be affected if you think you are not doing what a mum should be doing or are not doing it well.

'A quote that I read once really resonated with me. "It is so easy to compare your worst with someone else's best." This made me realise it is not worth comparing myself to other mums or to what society expects of me because the truth is everyone in the world has bad days as well when even they don't feel adequate or confident in their abilities. I just remind myself of all the great things I have done and don't let a moment get to me too personally otherwise it will crush my spirit.'

— Veronica (33), mum to Oscar (seven)

While it is okay to feel uncertain or unsure at times, it is important that you continue to believe in yourself and what you are capable of. You are taking on a role that comes with a massive amount of responsibility and so there will naturally be moments where you don't feel entirely confident. After all, you're desperately trying to be a great mum who is doing her best to shape her child's wellbeing.

'I admit I am an insecure person on a good day, so it doesn't take much to make me lose my confidence. What I have done to help me bounce back faster is write a list of all the things I am good at and proud of. That way, when I do feel down, or something has got to me, by looking at the list it takes me less time to reclaim my self-confidence.'

— Olga (36), mum to Lianna (two)

Listed below are some tips to make you feel as confident as you want to be.

Stop beating yourself up

How many times a day do you beat yourself up for the silliest things, such as, 'I shouldn't have eaten that', 'I should have spent more play time with the little one', 'I'll never be as rich/pretty/capable as that mum', 'I have more chin hairs than a goat', 'Who is that ugly person in the mirror?', 'I should spend more quality time with the kids', 'I should bring in more money to the household'? … The list goes on and on. But how many times do you actually say something positive and encouraging to yourself?

Now imagine all the negative comments reversed. 'I ate a great balanced diet today', 'Ben and I read three books today instead of one', 'I am grateful to be financially okay',

'I scrub up okay with a bit of lippie and mascara', 'Yes, these jeans still fit me', 'I've been budgeting really well lately and saved enough for a family treat/new shoes'. It makes a difference to how you feel, doesn't it?

As soon as you recognise your negativity, change your comments so that they are more positive and empowering. Having a more positive attitude towards yourself is the first step to regaining your confidence. If you continue to hear something long enough, you start to believe it. So make it positive and constructive. Don't put yourself down.

Don't let doubt get in the way of reality

Doubt is a natural feeling that will always arise when you have lost your confidence or find yourself in a new situation or unfamiliar position. Before you know it, doubt takes over and lets into your head that negative voice that makes you doubt yourself, what you are doing and the choices you are making.

You are not alone. Everybody can lose faith at different points in their lives. This is because it is all too easy to tell ourselves we can't do something before we even have a go. Imagine if you truly believed you were someone who could achieve anything. There would be no stopping you. The mind will do whatever you tell it to do — positive or negative. So you have to be conscious of what thoughts you feed your mind.

The best way to handle doubt before it affects your confidence levels is to recognise that doubt is only a perspective. It doesn't stop you from doing something unless you let it. Doubt is simply the way part of your mind checks to see if you are sure you want to do something. So when thoughts threaten to stop you from progressing in any way, remind yourself of the facts and continue moving forward.

Bring more confidence into your life

Have you noticed how much lighter you feel after an interaction with a really bubbly, happy person who clearly loves life? You immediately want to shed the slack attitude, tiredness or bitterness you have and instead radiate that uplifting spirit as well. It's contagious.

The same applies if you are looking for more confidence. Spend more time with confident women and you'll come home inspired and motivated. When you are drained and stressing out over potential mastitis or whether the baby has an infection, you don't want to hear depressing tales of worse things to come.

If there is a mum you admire from your mothers' group, work, neighbourhood or circle of acquaintances, try to spend more time with them. They can share some tips about how they keep it together and some of their confidence will naturally rub off on you.

'There was this mum who was running a top business, looked amazing all the time, had sexy chemistry with her husband and a well-behaved child. In the beginning I did not want to be anywhere near her because it reminded me of everything I didn't have. But I changed my attitude and spent more time with her so I could learn what it took to look, feel and be as confident as she was. I discovered she was a women just like me.

The difference was that she genuinely believed everything she touched would turn to gold. That is a magic ingredient to her confidence levels. I started to feel inspired and more confident about what skills I had and what I could achieve. I learnt I could be as confident as I allowed myself to be.'

— Deanna (30), mum to Ruri (four) and Max (two months)

Trust yourself

There will never be a shortage of people willing to tell you what to do or who think they know it all. In this day and age, advice, help, information, resources and experts are all at our fingertips. But when you have just had a baby, too much of the above can simply make things harder and more confusing.

Rather than trying to process all the overwhelming and sometimes conflicting information being thrown at you, try taking in only what suits you best. Trust your own intuition and feelings. What works for the next person might not work for you. Trust that you know your newborn and yourself better than anyone. If you feel like you should be doing something different, do it.

'When I was at the hospital after giving birth my baby was crying every 45 minutes. I wasn't producing enough milk, but the midwives kept pushing me to persevere with breastfeeding. I felt in my heart that my baby was starving. He continued crying like this until we got home. As soon as I got home I tried breastfeeding first, followed by a formula top-up and he was so content and sleeping longer — and it did not affect my breastfeeding. I went on to breastfeed for twelve months. I should have listened to my gut from the beginning, but because it was my first child I trusted the experts.'

— Irene (33), mum to Romeo (one)

Ditch the guilt

Let's face it, now that we are mothers, we are going to feel guilty and/or inadequate about one thing or another for the rest of our lives. 'I shouldn't send him to childcare', 'I should feed him more vegetables', 'I should have breastfed for longer', 'I should do attachment parenting', etc., etc. And this is all in the first few months. Just wait until they can talk and actually verbalise the blame for the things we did or did not do!

'When Jessie was two I left her with my mum so I could go and buy shoes for a function. Jessie went to climb the pram from the front while the brakes were not on. The pram slipped back and Jessie rammed her two top teeth right up into her gums. She needed surgery to have them removed altogether. And now she won't have teeth in the most obvious place in her mouth until the second ones come through when she is at least six.

I felt horrible. I left her to get shoes, of all things. For a really long time all I could think of was that if she was with me this wouldn't have happened. But, after speaking with many other mums, I've just accepted that kids will be kids and will fall, bump and bruise themselves whether we are with them or not. And, unfortunately, we can't be with them every second of the day to protect them. It's just not life.'

— Serena (34), mum to Jessie (four)

If you find yourself feeling guilty, just remind yourself that you had good intentions and with all your heart did not mean for anything negative to happen as a result. After all, this is life and sometimes kids will get hurt.

You can also think about what triggers the guilt and make a conscious effort to do something about it so that you don't feel guilty next time. For example, you could freeze extra portions of vegetables so that a nutritious meal is always available. You could childproof your home more so accidents are less likely. Or you could bring a favourite toy or blanket to childcare or the minder's house so you know that your baby is more comfortable.

Finally, get over it and move on! There are more important things to worry about and it is not worth the energy sweating the small stuff.

Acknowledge your emotions

Sometimes you or your baby will have a bad day and you will feel absolutely shattered. You might even be so desperate that you need to have a big, fat cry in front of your child. Accept that it is unrealistic to expect you are always going to be a calm, poised individual who has her emotions under control — especially while you are sleep deprived and still trying to manage fluctuating hormones.

It is okay if your child sees you break down sometimes — you are only human. But it's also reassuring for your child when they see you get over it. So, after a meltdown, pick yourself up, put on a strong face and smile so your baby is reassured everything is okay. Alternatively, if your baby is frightened or distressed by seeing you like this, either try to avoid letting them see you this upset or get someone to help you out while you pull yourself together.

Importantly, don't let your emotions affect your overall confidence in your abilities to be an amazing mum or woman. We are all entitled to have 'a moment', as long as for the majority of the time our emotions are reasonable. However, if these breakdowns are not isolated cases and if you are experiencing any form of depression, you should see your doctor.

Enjoy the moment

Building self-confidence doesn't always have to be hard work. It can actually be quite easy. Slow down and take time to really digest everything your beautiful baby is doing. He or she might be reacting to music, holding the bottle independently, grasping a toy really well, or just be an overall content, happy baby. All these milestones should make you feel proud and confident of the individual you are responsible for shaping.

Reflect on the great things you shared together during the day and write them down. When you do feel your confidence slipping a little, read the list and remind yourself of these things and that you should be proud and confident that you are indeed doing a wonderful job.

Fake it until you make it

Teachers, kinder or childcare professionals can command respect with a tone of voice or clap of a hand. If we stress out with one child, surely they must be frazzled at times when dealing with a roomful of loud, smelly, fast individuals who all need something at the same time! But they never let the kids smell fear or weakness. The same applies to lion tamers — it's not like they run and hide when they are faced with a hungry lioness. And we have to do the same.

If you want to be more confident in yourself, start acting more confident. Babies are highly intuitive and can pick up on our cues. Pretend you know what you are doing and that you are in control. In turn, your baby will feel calmer and safer, knowing that you have their best interests at heart. And if your baby is calm, you will be calm enough to actually work out what to do next.

So stay calm and act in control while you figure out the next step. It will become easier to do each time, and before long you really will be calm and in control!

CHAPTER 6

... is for 'Diet'

This chapter is not about obtaining the Hollywood size 0 body so you can prance around in 6-inch heels and skinny jeans ten days after giving birth. This chapter is about recognising the benefits of a great diet and how it can influence a mum's energy, self-esteem and confidence. It provides some practical ways to easily and realistically get your diet on track. A celebrity personal trainer or chef is not required.

I totally understand that being a new mum or busy mum means that you don't necessarily have the luxury of eating properly, let alone have the energy to even care about what you eat. Sometimes you feel grateful to get through a coffee before it goes cold and eat three chocolate biscuits by 1.30 p.m., far less find the time for a nutritional, sit-down breakfast, lunch and dinner, plus snacks.

But eating well does affect the way we feel and function. There are so many reasons for a new mum to maintain good nutrition. For starters, a good diet will give you the energy to tackle your long day and night, will help you sleep better (when you do get the chance to sleep) and will give your body what it needs to be as healthy as possible. As an added benefit, it will be easier to maintain a healthy weight as your internal systems will be working at their best — which means you'll get the chance to wear your favourite jeans again.

While the aim of a good diet is not simply to lose weight, the majority of new mums we spoke to all agreed that their weight affected their self-esteem and influenced their confidence levels. All the women also said that once they lost a bit of weight and could fit into their pre-baby clothes they really started to feel good about themselves. If your weight was something you were conscious of before, you will probably still be conscious of it now. Don't stress out or beat yourself up about it, though. After all, you do have other, bigger priorities. Just remember that one of the benefits of paying some attention to your diet will mean you shift some unnecessary kilos and regain your confidence in return.

As everyone will remind you, it takes nine months to put the weight on so it will take some time to get it off. But don't neglect yourself in the meantime. Eating too many high-fat and high-sugar foods can make you feel sluggish, tired and add to your feelings of being overweight.

Getting your diet in order after having a baby doesn't have to be hard, expensive or time consuming. It just comes down to being prepared, organised and motivated. It takes no more effort to eat well than it does to make the wrong choices.

Preparation

Once you have the all clear from your doctor to pay attention to things like diet, prepare yourself for a healthy eating regime. You can start by writing a list of some handy, nutritional foods and snacks that are easy to access and require little or no preparation. Foods such as rice crackers, canned tuna, muesli bars, yoghurt, canned lentils or vegetables, pre-cut salads, low-fat microwave meals, etc.

Next, make sure your cupboards are stocked with more of the good stuff and less of the bad and the not so good. This way, you have your resources on hand. When you don't have anything nutritious in the cupboard it is all too easy to give in to temptation. So stock up at the supermarket and then, when you get a chance to eat, it will be easy to reach out for something healthy.

Organisation

Some days are just mayhem. You get to the end of the day and you have no idea where the hours went and what exactly you did. On days like these it is really hard to get a chance to eat properly. Just when you have put the baby down for a nap, returned some calls, hung out the washing, cleared the kitchen sink and are ready for a bite to eat, the baby wakes up, ready for the next round. Your window of opportunity is gone and it seems virtually impossible to sit down to a balanced meal.

'When I got home from the hospital, I didn't lose any more weight; contrary to all the myths I read about breastfeeding helping you lose weight. I spoke to my mum, who was a bit of a diet junkie and we wrote down everything I was eating on a typical day.

I was overdoing it on too many high-calorie snacks and missing out on key food groups like fruit and protein. The best tip she gave me was to put some basic foods in a bowl on the kitchen bench so that when I walked past the kitchen I could grab something that would help me feel fuller for longer and would be better for me than four chocolate biscuits.

So every day I filled that bowl with nutritious food to get through. I would put snacks such as three fruits, a yoghurt, some vegetable crudités, some bread, two hard-boiled eggs, some leftover dinner and an individual pack of rice crackers. I also filled a 1-litre jug of water. The deal was that before I even thought about reaching for sugar-loaded treats I had to get through these foods that my body needed to properly get through the day and replenish after breastfeeding. I didn't miss the sugar treats, because I was still as busy as ever, but I did feel much better about myself and it was easy because everything was at my fingertips and ready to eat. Because I spent a few minutes being organised, I started to shift a few kilos without even noticing and started to feel good again.'

— Krista (33), mum to Jackson (six) and Gabrielle (three)

It really is easy to put out on the kitchen bench some healthy foods that you can scoff on the next day whenever you happen to be walking past. It helps so much because you don't have to think too hard about what you are eating or procrastinate over how long it takes to prepare. Instead you can just grab what's available. There is nothing to think about.

Motivation

It does take discipline to be healthy and you need to hold on to what will motivate you. Surely you don't want to be wearing your maternity clothes for another nine months after giving birth? I don't know about you, but after having the baby I could not stand the sight of maternity clothes any more and was seriously tempted to burn them all.

'A few weeks after giving birth I put all my maternity clothes in a box and I pulled out my pre-baby clothes. The first thing I did was hang up my favourite pair of jeans on the door to remind myself of what I wanted and to motivate me. For me, fitting into them was going to make me feel good about myself again.'

— Moira (34), mum to Steven and Jordan (four)

I tried on my old wardrobe until I found some basics that I could get away with. Every week or so I would try on a few key pieces and make a mental note of how much longer it would take me to fit into them. I knew I had two choices:

1. To accept my new weight and buy new clothes or settle for wearing four items of clothing from my existing wardrobe.
2. To pay attention to my diet and reclaim a whole new wardrobe. Even though the clothes were technically old, I hadn't worn them for nearly a year, so they all looked nice and shiny to me.

The first option didn't appeal, so I chose to spend some time paying attention to my diet and within nine months I had lost all the weight. I was not obsessed with my diet; I just made a conscious effort to make better choices and spend some time preparing. To motivate myself I would try on old clothes and I treated myself to new outfits when I reached my goal weight.

'My husband supported me in my quest to be healthy and shift a few kilos. For every milestone I met, I was treated to things like lingerie, make-up, shoes. Having a supportive partner and some incentives was my motivation and the extra push that enabled me to concentrate on having a healthy diet. I just wanted to feel like my old sexy self again!'

— Jessica (40), mum to Elle (five) and Timothy (eighteen months)

Top tips for eating healthily

- To adjust to a new diet more easily, try changing just one habit a week until you have a fairly balanced diet.

- Start a circle of friends who also want to have a better diet and encourage and motivate one another.

- Make sure your pantry is well stocked with nutritious food so that there is less temptation to eat fatty, sugary foods.

- Plan the night before so that you have some nutritional snacks on hand for the next day.

- Don't feel guilty about spending time on your diet. A good diet will nourish your body and assist with the post-baby recovery process, making you a stronger, healthier mum.

- Make extra dinner so that it serves as your ready to heat and eat lunch.

- When you cut up a salad for dinner, put aside some cut vegetables for the next day. All you then have to do is add a can of tuna/beans/protein and some dressing for a healthy lunch.

- Don't buy sugary or fat-laden treats. If they are not in the house, you won't eat them.

- Learn more about the diet and nutritional requirements that are right for your weight, lifestyle and goals. If you are armed with the knowledge, then it is easier to make the right choices.

- Treat yourself every so often so that you don't feel deprived.

- Give yourself an incentive or reward that is not food related for every milestone you achieve.

- Increase your fluid levels. Sometimes we eat when we are actually just thirsty, so try drinking water before eating.

- A breastfeeding mum should not deny or deprive herself of food when hungry, but try to choose snacks that are better for your health.
- Don't pressure yourself to lose weight by a certain timeframe. Lower your expectations and start slowly until you adjust.
- Focus more on making a balanced eating plan part of your lifestyle, then the rest of the benefits — such as losing a few kilos — will follow naturally.
- Even the perfect diet will not relieve the fatigue a new mum can feel, so make sure you rest when possible. It's easier to concentrate on eating habits when you are not exhausted.
- Don't worry if you have the occasional setback in your eating habits. Sometimes you will go out to eat, someone else will cook or you will wake up really hungry. That's life. Fortunately, we eat on average eighteen meals a week, plus snacks, so we can always make up for it by monitoring the rest of the meals we consume.
- If you need extra support and information, speak to your doctor or consider a dietician or weight management program that is equipped to assist new mothers or breastfeeding mothers.

CHAPTER 7

... is for 'Exercise'

You're tired, hungry, dirty and emotional, all by 11 a.m. Welcome to the demands of motherhood — until you get the hang of things anyway! The last thing on your mind right now is exercising. However, after your post-natal check-up, exercise could be one of the best things for your mind and body.

Regardless of all the pressures and challenges motherhood brings, there will come a moment when you look in the mirror and wonder how and if it is possible to regain your pre-pregnancy shape and fit into your favourite jeans again. Unless you are genetically blessed, it is totally normal and incredibly common to look like you are still pregnant shortly after giving birth. It can take weeks before you start recognising some muscle tone or flatness. Your ripped six-pack of abs is just a distant memory.

'Would you believe, 48 hours after giving birth I had two hospital visitors "politely" tell me that I still had a tummy and I should look at wearing a girdle (!!!). I was flabbergasted and close to kicking them out of my room. Too shocked to respond I made a mental note to revisit the pamphlet on stomach exercises the midwives had left me earlier that day.'

— Christabelle (29), mum to Luanda (three months)

The good news is that Mother Nature will help your insides get back in order. Based on a normal pregnancy and delivery, after about six weeks your uterus will have contracted close to its former size. The bad news is that your muscles are pretty weak, your fitness levels nowhere near what they were beforehand, and you can still see the 36 packets of chocolate biscuits and 8 kilos of gourmet Swiss cheese from the days of 'eating for two' hovering around your mid-section, butt and thighs. To get back in shape, you will need to exercise.

Depending on how you are feeling, the amount of exercise you did before and during pregnancy, the kind of birth you had and other variables your doctor can chat to you about, you may need to wait until after your six-week check-up before you start exercising. However, in normal circumstances, some pelvic floor and abdominal exercise is recommended from when you are in hospital. The hospital will usually provide you with this information before you are discharged.

Don't pressure yourself to exercise until you feel ready. Listen to your body and remember that the initial weeks are all about resting, recovering, bonding with your baby (see 'B ... is for Babymoon') and finding a routine that works. There are enough challenges to deal with in the beginning without feeling extra pressure to jump straight into your jeans. But when you are ready, start to slowly incorporate an exercise routine into your new lifestyle. Be realistic and don't do too much too soon.

Exercise does not have to involve a marathon or a bucketload of sweat to be beneficial. It just needs to be consistent. Your mind and body will reap rewards from regular, gentle exercise. As your heart rate increases and your body releases endorphins, you feel energised, invigorated, healthy and happier — and a little less flabby. If you exercise outdoors with the baby, the fresh air and surrounds can soothe, stimulate and relax them as well, so both of you benefit.

Ten reasons why exercise is good for you

1. It tones up the wobbly bits.
2. It clears your head.
3. It reduces stress levels.
4. It releases happy endorphins.
5. It's cheap.
6. Your increased metabolism will speed up weight loss and get you back in shape.
7. It gives baby a chance to hear, see and sense different things if you exercise together.
8. It gives you more energy and helps restore your pre-pregnancy fitness levels.
9. It gets you away from housework.
10. You will recover and heal faster after giving birth.

'As much as I dread going to the gym, the hardest part is just getting there. Actually working out is easy and makes me feel happy (and probably relaxed because I temporarily run away from everyone and everything). I find I zone out and come back to my family with a bit more energy and calmness. I force myself to just do it and then I treat myself to a coffee in the gym's café so it was all worthwhile.'

— Melanie (38), mum to Jasper (eight) and Monica (four)

The following are a few helpful tips you should consider when planning your exercise program.

Be flexible

You might wake up with the best intentions to exercise that day, but find your plans go out the window because you are caught up cleaning projectile vomit off the carpet for the fourth time that day. Or you have an unexpected visitor drop in, or your baby is just too unsettled. If you have an off day, don't be too hard on yourself. In the early days of motherhood, the routine just keeps on changing and you don't always know what to expect. Flexibility is the key. Just make the most of any opportunity to exercise that you do get.

Make exercise part of your life

When your mind and body are ready for exercise, make an effort to incorporate it into your lifestyle by planning when and how you can fit it into your day. If you dedicate time for it, it will be easier to do and will become a habit. It is just as easy to meet a friend for a walking catch-up as it is to whine to them over a coffee that there is 'no time' for exercise.

Make your walk more interesting by going with a friend, stopping by the library or finishing off with a coffee at a café. Run errands on foot rather than by car. Don't forget to bring some baby supplies with you in case you get caught out.

Here are a few suggestions for other ways to incorporate exercise into your life.

- Walk during one of your baby's nap times.
- Run some errands or pick up the groceries on foot with the pram.
- Make a habit of walking to meet up with a friend.
- Have a regular exercise buddy so that you can motivate each other.

- Have some exercise DVDs on hand so that if it's raining outside you can still get the heart rate pumping. Even a 10-minute DVD is handy when you have limited time.
- Make a habit of doing more incidental exercise, such as taking the stairs instead of the lift and walking instead of driving.

'My community nurse told me to walk every day. Rain, hail or shine. It is healthy for you and the baby to get some fresh air and stimulation and to clear your head.'

— Dianne (26), mum to Alexia (five months)

Start slow

Don't expect too much too soon. It will take time to get back to your pre-pregnancy fitness levels and everyone bounces back at different rates. Give yourself time to reach your goals. Start slow until you feel you are ready to do more.

A gentle walk to the local coffee shop is a great start. As you get used to getting out of the house, start exploring a few different walking routes, depending on the amount of time you have. Work out a 20-minute route and then gradually increase it to an hour or so. Once you get into the habit of walking every day, vary your routine so that you go further or faster. If you are really enthusiastic, motivated and ready to do more, wear a pedometer to track your progress and set goals, strap on some leg weights, walk uphill or try jogging. Remember, you will eventually be able to return to doing the exercise you used to do before you had a baby, but you will need to ease into the exercises and the intensity levels over time.

Get some help

Everyone has different opinions on how much you should exercise and how soon to start getting your body and fitness back to normal. After speaking to your doctor, you can also consult other health experts. Professionals like a personal trainer or exercise instructor can provide information regarding women's health and work with you to tailor a program to suit your needs, goals, routine and expectations.

There are many gyms and exercise groups that are actually baby friendly. Some gyms have child-minding facilities, while some exercise groups encourage you to bring your baby to the sessions. Your local community may even have special classes that incorporate the baby and pram as part of the exercise routine. These can be ideal, as you learn practical ways to exercise now you're a mother; i.e. lunges holding onto the pram bar, or squats while holding the baby.

If you prefer to exercise on your own, try to get a reliable babysitter so that you can regularly dedicate some time to focus on an exercise session without worrying about your child. Exercising on your own can be a refreshing outlet to clear your head and restore your emotions so you feel more balanced when you go back to baby. It also makes it possible to try exercise classes such as Pilates, yoga or group sports, where you can socialise and exercise simultaneously.

Ideal exercises for a new mum

- Brisk walking
- Cycling
- Yoga
- Pilates
- Swimming/water aerobics

- Basic strength training
- Low-impact aerobics
- Stomach and pelvic floor exercises
- Mum and baby exercise sessions

Top exercise tips

- Make sure you consult with your doctor before commencing any new exercise regime.
- Start slowly.
- Wear a supportive bra and shoes.
- Chat to your local midwife if you are concerned about exercise affecting breastfeeding.
- Drink plenty of water so you don't get dehydrated.
- If you exercise with your baby, make sure you bring essential supplies such as nappies, wipes, a baby toy and a snack so that you are prepared for any interruptions.
- Time your exercise around feeding or sleep routines so that you are more organised and less stressed.
- Don't be too hard on yourself in the beginning, because it will take time to get to pre-pregnancy fitness levels.
- There are plenty of experts available who can answer questions about exercise for new mums.
- Exercise can actually be a fun way to bond with your baby and socialise with others.
- Eat regular, healthy meals so that your body is properly nourished and provides the energy you need to exercise.

- To feel the long-term benefits of exercise, try to exercise three to five times a week.
- Exercise does not have to be vigorous or too intense.
- If exercise makes you feel faint or short of breath, stop immediately.
- Listen to your body and don't push yourself too far too soon.
- Set some short-term and long-term goals so you can work towards improving your results.
- Vary the routine so you don't get bored.

CHAPTER 8

... is for 'Friendships'

New mothers really benefit from a few key, honest friendships to assist them on their journey. As a new mum, the majority, if not all, of your time is spent attending to the needs of your newborn. As your child grows, you will continue to devote an enormous amount of time and energy to your family, partner and household needs and this can, at times, be really difficult, stressful and draining. You might find there is little time to address what *you* want and no one there to attend to your needs the way you attend to others. That's why a supportive network of friends is vital.

As I've said before, you are going to have days where you are seriously sleep deprived, hormonally imbalanced, struggling with a cranky baby, affected by the isolation and mundane routine you are faced with and wishing for a brighter situation. This is when you need someone to talk to and share your feelings with. Friends who won't judge you, who will understand you and who are there to lend a sympathetic ear are invaluable. Of course, many women have a husband or mother figure they can vent to. But what do you do if your husband or partner is too busy working and stressed with their own problems, or if your mum can't be there for you when you need her most? You turn to your friends.

The right friends can instantly make you feel better after a hormonal outburst and will help you find your sense of humour when everything seems impossible. At this point in your life, you may find it's the friends who have children of their own whom you want to spend more time with because they naturally understand what you are going through. Other mothers who have been through it all before with their children will make you realise you are not alone and that there is light at the end of the bleak tunnel. While they won't necessarily solve the world's problems for you, just having them around to share tips and views with will allay any concerns you have.

'It's a relief to know that I have a few key friends, with children of their own, who I can completely let my guard down with and be myself. I am a real woman who has good days, bad days and some sad, stressed-out days. I don't want to put up a front and pretend that everything is wonderful when sometimes it really isn't. This is just another pressure I don't need.'

— Emily (32), mum to Charlotte (six) and Matilda (two)

'When I met my new mums' group for the first time, I was having a particularly bad day. I'd recently experienced depression and was going through some serious marital and financial problems. When the midwife asked us individually how we were travelling I just broke down in hysterical tears in front of all these guarded mums because it was the first time someone had asked me how I was. Well, that broke the ice.

After that, it wasn't uncommon for some of the other mums to be having a problem or bad day of their own that warranted their own public meltdown. We were all honest and admitted motherhood is not all it's cracked up to be all the time. As a result we have a genuine friendship six years on and we understand one another. Nobody judges. We are just here to enjoy each other's company, genuinely support one another, share our ups and downs and watch our children grow. They are my therapy group who let me vent, laugh and cry and I couldn't cope without them.

I wish all mums had real friendships to share (and survive) the journey with.'

— Maria (38), mum to Dean (four) and Peter (one)

Without friendships, life as a mum can be isolating, ordinary and at times depressing. Without friendships you won't have someone to relate to who can remind you that they too have gone through similar issues and that you are not alone. A friend's encouragement and support can give you a sense of confidence and more positive self-esteem.

Existing friendships may strengthen or weaken as the dynamics of the relationship change. You may even crave new 'mum' friends in your life because your old friends live too far away, are busy climbing corporate ladders or are enjoying a totally different lifestyle to yours, particularly if they are single and childless. Sometimes motherhood will create a gap in existing friendships as you find you have less in common.

If you don't have many friends whom you can relate to, you might have to venture out of your comfort zone to start forging new friendships. If you are normally shy or reserved, this is especially daunting. Fortunately, there are so many ways you can make new friends. Good places to start are community groups such as playgroups and mothers' groups, library sessions, mums and bubs activities; activity sessions; ex-work/school mates; playdates; friends of friends; and the internet.

Community groups

Many communities run activities that welcome mothers and their children. For instance, your community library may run a story-time session. Here the children gather to listen to and discuss a story, while the mums can enjoy a hot drink and some light banter. These sessions are normally free and provide a perfect excuse to start chatting to other mums.

Some communities encourage new mothers in the area who have all given birth to their children around the same time to meet. They will host a term of free discussion groups at the local community centre where the mums can gather with their children to learn about aspects of parenting. At the same time, friendships are formed. At the end of the term, mums can decide if they would like to pursue a friendship and continue running their own mothers' group. Normally, a mums' group will arrange to catch up at a local park, café or someone's home for morning tea. Kids have a play, mums let off a little steam and have a laugh, and everyone leaves feeling a little lighter.

If your community does not facilitate a traditional mothers' group, your council will have a directory of playgroups in your area that you could look at joining. For a small fee you can attend a group that welcomes children in the same age bracket as your child and encourages friendships and discussions between mothers. If there aren't any in your area, you could speak to your council about how to start your own. Your local church or community hall may also run similar groups.

Activity sessions

There are many activities you can consider joining that not only stimulate your child's development but also provide an opportunity for you to meet other mums. For example, there are music classes, arts and craft sessions, gym classes, dance classes and more. Many require a joining and attendance fee. The activities are often broken into sessions, such as parent and child joint involvement followed by free play for the kids and coffee and tea for the parents. Local papers, classified advertisements and directory listings can direct you to a suitable activity in your neighbourhood. Activity sessions give you a chance to get to know people you would not have come into contact with otherwise.

Ex-work/school mates

It is easy to lose contact with friends from school or people you used to work with. However, you might find that in your new life as a mother there are different things to talk about and new experiences to share. Motherhood can provide an excuse to reconnect with old friends, particularly if they are parents as well. Next time you come across an old friend, don't be afraid to ask to catch up for a coffee. You never know how you might get along now, years on, and how they could actually prove to be a wonderful friend to have in your life.

'I was working with this nice girl many years ago, but when we each left the company we did not keep in touch. We just didn't have enough of a bond to warrant continuing contact. Several years later, we bumped into each other at the doctor's surgery — both eight months pregnant. We decided to swap numbers and 'catch up'. After nearly four years of 'catching up', she is now one of my closest friends. Back then, I never, ever would have thought we would be in each other's lives in the future, but now I expect to be friends with her for many decades to come. Her friendship is a great source of support and I love her dearly.'

— Larissa (38), mum to Sarita (four) and Zachary (three months)

Playdates

This is an easy way to meet other mums. All you are required to do is set up a playdate for your child with a neighbour, kinder/childcare buddy, friend of a friend or familiar acquaintance. This gives you the opportunity to chat on a more personal level and see if there is enough common ground to start a friendship and continue meeting. If you have children the same age, you will find there is more to talk about as you dissect common milestones and issues you're both experiencing at similar times.

Online world

Online networks can be a lifeline for those of us who have moved to a new area, are living in small communities or are just too shy to start a conversation with strangers. You can ignite virtual friendship with others who can provide support, tips, regular interaction and friendly comradeship.

The online world continues to grow and almost daily there is a new support group available for mums who want to connect with other mums for friendship, advice and understanding. There are online groups you can join, forums you can participate in and live chats you can have with others just like you. The online environment allows you to hold onto some anonymity as you openly chat about issues and things you are going through that you would like a 'friend' to listen to.

Online worlds are an invaluable resource when you are having a moment at 4 a.m., don't have access to a live network of friends and just want to let your guard down to anyone who will listen. You can get advice from experts and share stories with other mums. Some groups will even connect you with mums who live in your local area so that there is also the opportunity to meet in person. Most online resources are free to participate in.

✳✳✳

Having friends in your life to share concerns, offer support and laugh with will make you feel confident in the knowledge that you are genuinely not alone and that there are people other than your partner and family with whom you can share the journey.

CHAPTER 9

G

... is for 'Goal setting'

'You got to be careful if you don't know where you're going, because you might not get there.'

— Yogi Berra

Once you become a mum you immediately get absorbed in all the day-to-day activities and very quickly ignore the most important things in life. You are managing sleep deprivation, breastfeeding, perhaps other children, household chores, family commitments, relationships and maybe also work and financial pressures. No wonder you have zero time for yourself, inadequate quality time with your loved ones and not a moment to think about how you want things to pan out in the future. That's where goal setting can help.

Goal setting is an effective strategy for new mums who are ready to and want to feel in control of themselves, motherhood and their journey. As a mum, you have the most challenging role in life. Not only are you likely to be the main lifeline for a little person who depends on you 24/7, but you are also juggling your own issues, such as isolation, lack of self-esteem, boredom, guilt, emptiness and uncertainty. You struggle to find energy for your own needs because you are too busy taking care of everyone else first and trying to fit everything in.

When you feel inundated and as if you're craving direction on how to be more organised and fulfilled, it is time to review key areas of your life and work out what matters to you most. What do you truly want and expect from yourself and your life? Identifying this will crystallise your goals and what's important to you. Then you can feel more motivated and inspired as you start work on achieving a more satisfying life, because you have a clearer idea of where you will end up as a result.

New mums should only concentrate on goal setting when they feel mentally prepared and physically recovered from giving birth. There is no need to do more than just recover and bond with baby in the first six weeks or so. Thereafter, goal setting will play a part in building your confidence, time management skills and your ability to feel in control of the next stage.

Goal setting is all about establishing definite, measurable and time-targeted objectives. Everyone has different things that they want from life, but often goals are neglected if they are too general or unrealistic. Mums can have goals under a number of umbrellas including:

- Family
- Health
- Financial
- Business
- Career
- Relationships
- Emotional
- Spiritual
- Lifestyle
- Happiness

Goal setting can be as simple or as elaborate as we like. Here are three different ways you can go about goal setting to suit different lifestyles, personalities and needs. They are equally effective. The main thing is that you end up with specific, realistic goals you can measure.

Six-month goal planner

On your own, armed with just your notebook, visit a comfortable environment where you are unlikely to be interrupted, such as a library or local coffee shop, and settle yourself in for a 30-minute brainstorming session.

Write down key headings such as Personal, Family & Friends, Parenting, Spiritual, Career, Finance, Health & Fitness, and anything else that matters to you. Reflect on each heading and consider where you are now and where you would like to see yourself in six months' time.

Select the three areas that matter most and write down one goal for each area. For each of these three goals write down what you will do to get a little closer to it in one month, three months and six months. By doing this you will have clearly outlined the three most important goals you want to achieve in the next six months and what you can start doing this month to get a little closer to what you want.

Keep these goals visible as a reminder, and when you are ready, you can review and reconsider other important areas of your life for which you would like to set a goal and plan for.

For example, three key areas of a new mum's life might be: Health & Fitness, Career and Wellbeing. The three respective goals may read something like this:

Six-month goal planner

GOAL	1 MONTH PLAN	3 MONTH PLAN	6 MONTH PLAN
Health & Fitness			
• Complete a 6 km walk–run marathon	• Register for the marathon • Enlist a friend to support/motivate/join me • Walk 3 km x 4 times per week	• Lay-by new trainers suitable for marathon • Start getting family to sponsor marathon • Walk–run 5 km x 3 times per week	• Collect trainers • Complete marathon • Collect sponsors' funds • Register for the 10 km walk–run marathon
Career			
• Get paid for writing articles	• Start a blog • Write 3 blog entries per week on topics that interest me	• Submit free articles for publication to have work published and beef up portfolio with 12 published pieces • Attend 1 networking event	• Send introductory email/letter to 20 avenues with sample of work • Research, prepare and submit 6 story ideas to key avenues that commission articles

Wellbeing			
• Feel rested and not sleep deprived	• Lie down for 30 minutes every afternoon when the baby is having a sleep	• Arrange a babysitter/ family member for 2 hours per week so that I can have uninterrupted relaxing time • Start a weekly relaxing ritual where I completely 'switch off' everything when the baby goes to bed for the night so I can bathe, moisturise, have a warm drink, read and sleep	• Baby routine to include daily quiet time • Continue weekly 2 hour babysitter arrangement • Continue weekly relaxing routine • Swap babysitting duties with friend for 3 hours per week

SMART *theory*

The SMART theory is a well-documented and formal way some people go about setting goals. SMART stands for:

- Specific — goals must be specific in their detail.
- Measurable — goals must be measurable in quantity, time and cost.
- Achievable — goals must be achievable within a timescale.

- Relevant — goals must be relevant.
- Timescale — goals must have a timescale otherwise they will never be finished.

A great benefit of using the SMART approach is that you really think through exactly what you want to achieve and tighten up that goal. It is not enough to say, 'I want to lose weight.' In the SMART approach you will say, 'I want to be 5 kilos lighter in three months and I want to do this by shedding half a kilo a week for the next twelve weeks with a balanced diet and 30 minutes of exercise per day.'

Each goal becomes a lot clearer via the SMART approach. For example, if one of your goals is to afford to be a stay-at-home mum, the SMART approach will enable you to plan a way to get there: 'In six months' time, I want a part-time work-from-home job that uses my customer service skills and pays $30 per hour, so I will prepare my résumé, sign up to eight job boards and apply for one job per week.'

Easy goal setting

Start brainstorming a list of things you would like to accomplish. Put anything you can possibly think of on this list. The main thing is that you write down everything you want to be considered.

The next step is to review the list and figure out which specific goal is most likely to significantly change your life in the way you want. It you are confident that something is what you really want, it is easier to be motivated to achieve it.

Then, create your one-line mantra that you will post up somewhere you view constantly, such as the fridge, computer or change table. Every time you see it you need to repeat it aloud.

Write down what you can do this month to make the goal happen. By writing the smaller steps you need to do to get closer to that goal, you will have broken the goal down into mini, achievable steps that will make the process easier.

To keep the goal fresh in your mind, start the day with an action plan of what you can do that day to make your goal closer to becoming a reality. Then make that action plan one of your priorities for the day. Try not to put it off or you might find your day has disappeared and you have no time or energy left.

For example, your key goal might be to lose 5 kilograms. Your daily goal might be to take the baby on a walk. Your mantra would be: 'I will fit into my pre-pregnancy jeans this Christmas.'

***

As a new mum, it's far easier to focus on introducing one goal a month until it turns into an ongoing habit or is accomplished. When one goal is under control, you'll find it will be much easier to turn your energies to the next.

As well as one long-term goal at a time, you might want to set some simple daily goals. Daily goals are great because it is very easy to feel overwhelmed by everything you want to achieve — before you even get started, your day has disappeared! But a few simple daily goals can help you to stay on track and tick off the important things, one by one. For example, you might want to go for a walk, cook dinner, complete four loads of washing and iron all the shirts. Any mum will know that in the early days a list like this is far-fetched. So instead, break the list down into some simple goals: go for a 20-minute walk, prepare ingredients for dinner (so husband can help), and put one load of washing in the machine and on the line. Anything you achieve over and above this is a bonus.

'In the first few weeks of coming home from the hospital I just couldn't get my act together and found myself in pyjamas all day, feeling and looking awful. My self-esteem was pretty low, I felt a mess and out of control. My best friend got me sorted and convinced me to shower and beautify myself as one of the first things I do for the day. By making it my goal to clean myself up as a priority I had a much better, can-do attitude for the rest of the day. Not only did I start the day with a positive, happy mindset, but I also started to feel better about my appearance and what else I could do that day. I guess when I neglected myself, I neglected everything I was capable of doing.'

— Marianna (31), mum to Erin (one)

Things to remember about goal setting

- Set realistic expectations.
- Give yourself time before you start setting goals.
- Get out of your comfort zone.
- Clarify and properly specify what your goals are.

Benefits of goal setting

- It crystallises what you want to do with your life.
- It enables you to have better time management.
- It takes away that feeling of being overwhelmed by trying to manage everything.
- You feel more organised and in control.
- It gives you the opportunity to change direction in your life.
- It encourages practical ways to have better relationships.
- It makes achieving key milestones, such as losing pregnancy weight, easier.
- It's a practical way for you to become the best person you can be.

CHAPTER 10

... is for 'Humour in motherhood'

'Motherhood is the only place you get to experience heaven and hell at the same time.'

— Unknown

Hopefully you managed to find your sense of humour during pregnancy, because you are sure going to need it when you become a mother! If you were anything like the majority of pregnant women, you've already been through many changes and challenges that forced you to laugh at the reality of your new journey.

During pregnancy, perhaps you used to vomit with no warning, pee when you sneezed, needed help to shave your legs, grew out of your maternity clothes in your second trimester, cried and laughed in the same breath, left the house in mismatched shoes because you could no longer see your feet, or bumped into things because you managed to forget you had a belly.

Or perhaps your breasts grew bigger than your head, with nipples so dark and huge they might as well have glowed in the dark. You probably forgot things regularly, wanted sex 24 hours a day or not at all, needed a crane to get out of bed, hung out in the bathroom most of the time, and ended up with so many stretch marks that your stomach looked like a classroom blackboard at the end of the day. Let's not even discuss the haemorrhoids, hyper-sensitive sense of smell, leg cramps, unusual discharge, excessive flatulence and the never-ending belly comments. Yes, pregnancy was a barrel of laughs. And if you thought that was funny, wait until you see what's in store with motherhood.

If you don't lighten up about your experiences during and after pregnancy, you will not find the motivation to even get out of bed. You have some *wonderful* things to look forward to! Sarcasm intended. Your nipples will be so sore you won't want to feed your baby any more. Your breasts will be bigger than your entire child. You will probably have back fat for the first time in your life. Your milk will leak through your bra in public, that is if your breasts don't outright shower a stranger sitting in the next seat on the bus.

In addition, people — mainly family — will ignore you now that you have given birth. Your hair might fall out, sex — if it happens — will be interrupted, your periods will come back with a vengeance, and of course, those belly comments will just keep on coming. You will know by now that you have also lost the ability to string together a normal sentence and you have forgotten what interests, hopes and dreams you once had for yourself because you don't even know what day it is let alone who you are any more.

I don't know about you, but when I get together with some close friends going through a similar journey to mine (babies, toddlers, juggling motherhood and life), our conversations are always pretty similar. We talk, bitch, moan and eventually laugh about what on earth we have got ourselves into.

Talking and comparing notes tends to lessen the seriousness of some of our issues and we can relax a little, knowing that we are not alone in our desire to be the best mums and women we can and want to be. At the same time that we are going through our mini crises, there are hundreds more going through the same thing if not worse. Sometimes reminding ourselves of this can make us feel a little better, or at least not alone.

When we are stuck at home, isolated from life, battling with unreliable hormones, sleep deprivation, visitors, other kids and all the unknowns in between, it is all too easy to get depressed about a series of things that collectively build up and make you feel pretty low about yourself, your capabilities and your situation. It takes a lot of effort to find room to laugh at this point.

The problem lies in the fact that we are going through so many changes all at the same time. Soon enough they start to play havoc with our mind and how we function. It all gets too hard and we break down. As a new mum, you are usually battling a range of physical, mental and emotional changes.

Physically, you are so sleep deprived that as soon as you open your eyes you have a panic attack and look under your blanket because you honestly don't remember putting your child back into their cot after the 3 a.m. feed. Your nipples are so sensitive that it makes breastfeeding excruciating, and you reach a point where you are reluctant to even feed your child out of fear of the pain you inflict on yourself. You still feel like you have been hit by a bus eight days after giving birth, purely from the stress labour put on your body, and visitors seem to have taken up permanent residence in your living room.

You are also still hormonal and trying really hard to get to know your new baby, life and routine. It's only natural that you are going to be all over the place mentally and emotionally. Fortunately, time, experience, support and practice mean that everything does get better.

You will be relieved to learn that what stressed you out today will be a treasured story to tell tomorrow, surprisingly with a smile on your face. You might even find yourself laughing in public (while strangers cautiously avoid the weirdo with the pram talking to herself).

'It was just after 4 p.m. on a Friday, a week after we got home from hospital. The nurse called to see how we had all settled in. She asked me how breastfeeding was progressing. Did I have swollen boobs? Yes. Did I have red marks on them? Yes. Were they hard? Yes.

Oh no. I have mastitis and must get myself to the doctor immediately before I get a fever and get really sick, she explained.

It was impossible to see my family doctor, so I had to go to the dodgy after-hours clinic and beg to see any available doctor. When I went into the room and the old, quiet doctor asked what the problem was I explained, "I think I have mastitis." He asked me to take off my top and bra.

I believe I had size triple F breasts at this stage. I think that was a shock for him in itself. Then he had a feel of them. Would you believe he had the nerve to say, "Hmm, I'm not sure if it's mastitis." Not sure???!!!! I have just exposed my porno boobs to you, freaking out, and you are "not sure". I could have slapped him there and then.

Instead, I got him to write me up a prescription just in case my symptoms progressed and ran out of there as fast as I could. I gave him the show and feel of his life and I doubt he will forget the 29-year-old hottie with massive breasts offering him a feel.

Yes. I can laugh about it now and it is always a funny story for the dinner table, but I can assure you at the time it was far from funny.'

— Marika (30), mum to Tanea (one)

'All my life, my parents kept telling me how important it is to have a child. I was continuously told, "You haven't lived until you have one, life without one is selfish," etc. I believed them until I had my own child.

Three university degrees down the toilet because I could no longer work, boredom from cleaning the house and going to the park, constant worry that something would happen to the baby, loss of identity because no time or energy to look after myself anymore, financial restraints, travel restraints, etc., etc. It was crazy.

I definitely had some dark moments. Then I started wondering, "Why would my parents do this to me? Why would they wish something so mean on my life?" I trusted them. What I was going through as a mum was hard and horrible. Was this their idea of a bad joke? Well, if so, they got me there.

I can laugh now (only a very little) because it is true, I do get a lot of love back and I am learning to be a better, more holistic, responsible role model because of the fact I have kids. But there was (and still are) times when it was pretty hard to see the funny side of life as I now know it.'

— Melinda (36), mum to Jonathon (four) and Michael (one)

From talking to so many mums, I've learnt that our experiences are really not unique. We all get crushed, challenged and tested as a mother, and some days, battles and crises will suck the life out of you and any tiny fleck of humour you have left. On the bright side, you have two options: you can sink in self-pity, misery, self-doubt, low self-esteem and the 'why me' syndrome; or you can laugh about life's very amusing curve balls.

What seems to be so serious today can actually be funny after a good night's sleep and a therapy session with a friend. You can choose to let the typical things most mothers go through get in the way of enjoying life and motherhood, or you can take a moment — walk away if necessary — then put a smile on your face and remember some other hilarious moment in life and know that this too is just one of many, many more to come. At least you won't be short of stories to embarrass your child with on their 21st birthday!

Funny story about motherhood

Your clothes:

1st baby: You begin wearing maternity clothes as soon as your ob/gyn confirms your pregnancy.

2nd baby: You wear your regular clothes for as long as possible.

3rd baby: Your maternity clothes *are* your regular clothes.

Preparing for the birth:

1st baby: You practise your breathing religiously.

2nd baby: You don't bother because you remember that last time breathing didn't do a thing.

3rd baby: You ask for an epidural in your eighth month.

The layette:

1st baby: You pre-wash newborn's clothes, colour-coordinate them, and fold them neatly in the baby's little bureau.

2nd baby: You check to make sure that the clothes are clean and discard only the ones with the darkest stains.

3rd baby: Boys can wear pink, can't they?

Worries:

1st baby: At the first sign of distress

— a whimper, a frown — you pick up the baby.

2nd baby: You pick up the baby when her wails threaten to wake your firstborn.

3rd baby: You teach your three-year-old how to rewind the mechanical swing.

Dummy:

1st baby: If the dummy falls on the floor,

you put it away until you can go home and wash and boil it.

2nd baby: When the dummy falls on the floor,

you squirt it off with some juice from the baby's bottle.

3rd baby: You wipe it off on your shirt and pop it back in.

Nappies:

1st baby: You change your baby's nappies every hour,

whether they need it or not.

2nd baby: You change their nappy every two to three hours, if needed.

3rd baby: You try to change their nappy before others start

to complain about the smell or you see it sagging to their knees.

Activities:

1st baby: You take your infant to Baby Gymnastics,

Baby Swing, and Baby Story Hour.

2nd baby: You take your infant to Baby Gymnastics.

3rd baby: You take your infant to the supermarket and the dry cleaner.

Going out:

1st baby: The first time you leave your baby with a sitter, you call home five times.

2nd baby: Just before you walk out the door,

you remember to leave a number where you can be reached.

3rd baby: You leave instructions for the sitter to call only if she sees blood.

At home:

1st baby: You spend a good bit of every day just gazing at the baby.

2nd baby: You spend a bit of every day watching to be sure your older

child isn't squeezing, poking or hitting the baby.

3rd baby: You spend a little bit of every day hiding from the children.

Swallowing coins:

1st child: When first child swallows a coin,

you rush the child to the hospital and demand x-rays.

2nd child: When second child swallows a coin,

you carefully watch for the coin to pass.

3rd child: When third child swallows a coin

you deduct it from his allowance!

— Source unknown

CHAPTER 11

I

... is for 'Identity'

'The moment a child is born, a mother is also born. She never existed before. The woman existed, but the mother, never. A mother is something absolutely new.'

— Spiritual teacher Bhagwan Rajneesh

As your priorities in life change to include taking care of children, you are naturally immersed in motherhood. This is expected, natural and at times a joy. As someone who is now primarily a 'caretaker' or spends most of her time at home, you easily forget to invest time in taking care of your own sense of self. There is no time to do this in between the daily demands of motherhood. After all, you are too busy being the centre of someone else's universe to worry about your own needs.

'Nothing prepared me and nobody warned me that there was a seriously high possibility I wouldn't know myself once I left work to stay at home to rear a baby. I read all the parenting books, attended the mandatory pregnancy and birthing classes and chatted endlessly to other mothers before I had a child. Yet I had never heard of it, nor did it ever cross my mind, that I would feel lost as a person and question what I wanted from myself.

I don't know why no one mentioned this loss of identity to me. Especially seeing as the loss of identity ended up being one of my biggest challenges and no doubt a huge challenge for other mums also.

Now, when I meet a new mum to be, I subtly mention that this was a big change for me. I don't want to scare anyone. I just want them to know in advance that there is a personal period of adjustment some might have to go through, but that it is something that can be overcome. I wish someone warned me!'

— Esther (36), mum to Preston (four) and Rachel (one)

When you ignore your needs and spend time on everything and everyone but yourself, this is precisely when you start losing your identity. Keep it up and it won't take long before you will no longer know what you like, value, thrive on, enjoy or are passionate about. Nor will you be able to have a stimulating conversation with adults about matters other than kids. It is therefore vitally important that you maintain a strong sense of self and remember you are a mum and an individual with interests, dreams, passion, values and desires.

'Someone once told me that you just have to accept that for the first two months of your baby's life you are 'The Mother'. However, for me it was closer to the one-year mark. You will not be able to learn ballroom dancing, redecorate the bathroom with your own two hands or go for marathon bike rides. You are The Mother, so it is time you accept it, deal with it and dedicate yourself to being The Mother. It was also comforting to be told that you will eventually be able to get back into all — or at least most — of what you were into before your baby and be more than The Mother. It just takes a little extra effort to integrate these things into your new identity and life.'

— Tanya (32), mum to Toby (one)

Many mothers will go straight from being a professional employee to a homemaker. Pre-baby, many of us were working full time, with direct reports and budgets to manage, preparing for appraisals, negotiating bonuses, assisting in serious workplace issues, reading a hundred emails a day, attending dozens of meetings, involved in team-building exercises, and enlisting for extra-curriculum professional courses. Now, after having a baby, this same woman enters Groundhog Day.

You are home 24 hours a day. You get up at obscure hours of the night to breastfeed. You spend the majority of your time cooking, cleaning, bathing, settling, singing nursery rhymes, going to the park and always tending to the needs of a baby. Some days you can mix it up a bit by scrutinising different brands of formula or searching for the perfect nipple cream, but essentially, this is your life.

If you previously had a work-driven attitude and then become a mother, you can feel as though you are no longer part of the 'real' world as you knew it. You have gone from being acknowledged, recognised and rewarded for achieving things with your mind, expertise and business flair to cleaning, puréeing pumpkin and smelling like vomit. You were once a respected, educated, professional power-player in the boardroom, lived in suits and heels, sported freshly done hair and nails, and single-handedly delivered some pretty impressive, successful business projects. And now you probably can't even string a sentence together that doesn't include silly baby talk.

Of course you're going to feel like you no longer know yourself. You will question what happened to that woman and you may even panic that you only get ten emails a week as opposed to the ten emails an hour from your working life.

It is not until you are removed from your career that you realise how much your job shaped who you thought you were. When that is removed, and your accomplishments for the day are showering, brushing your teeth and dressing before midday, you may go through a time when you think, 'Who am I?' and 'Who have I become?' You don't want to go from being a professional worker to a stressed-out mother. You are not just defined by what you do. Motherhood becomes a time to learn *how* to be you.

Some women enter motherhood and relish a break from the workforce. They embrace motherhood and all the duties that come with it without any identity issues at all. Some might not experience a problem until many years later when they are ready to re-enter the workforce or no longer need to spend that much time at home with the kids. They find their new change of routine forces them into the community more than they have been accustomed to and that they have spent so much time dealing with the under-fives that they now feel inadequate, have low self-esteem and little confidence in their ability to communicate and function in an adult world. For years they have focused on taking care of the family and household needs, while ignoring their own potential, interests and abilities.

To avoid an identity crisis, it is paramount to recognise the warning signs and make an effort right from the start to keep and develop your own identity. It is in everyone's best interests if you make an effort to take care of your emotional and personal needs. You will be more balanced, happy and confident. In return, you will be a more positive, inspirational and well-adjusted mum and woman.

The following suggestions will help you get reacquainted with your needs and what shapes you as an individual, to remind you that you are more than a milk maker, nurturer, cleaner and 'Mother of All'. You are your own person, too.

Ten tips for avoiding an identity crisis

1. Take steps to start nurturing a passion. You won't have time to throw yourself in headfirst, but if you move towards spending more time on a personal interest, you will start to look forward to doing something that matters to you as an individual. This will shape your daily attitude and provide a break from being a mum, wife and everything else.

2. Recognise that you have needs as an individual and that it is not selfish to want to do something that matters to you personally. Be honest with yourself and admit what you need to do to make you happy and confident, because these admissions and actions will help you maintain your identity.

3. Make an effort to nurture a life that includes activities you enjoy and time with other friends and family. While at times this will feel impossible, it will prevent you from cocooning yourself in your own little bubble of babies, bottles and burping.

4. Accept that while being a mother is the heaviest and most involved responsibility you will have for life, it's not all you are cut out to do. It is easy to think that because being a mum is so tough and all consuming, it's impossible to consider doing anything else (or feel that you shouldn't even want to do anything else). While it will forever be a juggling act, you can get involved in something other than motherhood and you should.

5. Involve your partner or parents more with the children so that you don't fall into the trap of being or feeling like you are the only one who can satisfy a child's needs. Learn to let go so that you have more time to invest in yourself.

6. Don't think you have to be a perfect mum. This can be really stressful and tiring and can lead to burnout. Try being a real, happy mum

and balanced person and notice a difference in yourself and your happiness levels.

7. Talk to other mums in the same boat. Venting, sharing tips and support can bring comfort and inspiration.

8. Make a list of all the things you wanted to do before you became a mum and consider what you can now pursue. Perhaps you wanted to learn a new skill, start a business, embark on a hobby or enrol in a course. Now that you are out of the daily grind and are faced with a fresh start to a new journey, you can finally make fresh choices that matter to you as a person.

9. Don't isolate yourself. Make an effort to connect with society, get out of the house or interact with community groups, even if it's only online. This will give you the opportunity to keep in touch with others, voice concerns and get some support when you need it.

10. Take pride in all the work you do at home. Don't underestimate the value of your contribution to the family. Instead of feeling like you have 'downgraded' years of education and career developments to become a housewife, which can easily affect your self-esteem, remember why you chose to do this in the first place and that you now have the time to nurture and dote on your family more than you could if you were still working and immersed in career demands.

'My children are my life. They are my reason for almost everything I do … but I am still me, a woman, a dreamer, a procrastinator, a bad speller, a fashion tragic, a wishful singer, bad cook and everything else I was before Amelia was born.

I'm not selfish. I would never completely ignore my child to satisfy myself. But I do make the effort to remember to be myself.'

— Tracy (36), mum to Amelia (four) and Michelle (one)

In spite of all the changes and challenges we are faced with as a mother — the insecurities, the daily repetition, the constant guilt and the identity crisis — motherhood presents us with the opportunity to become an even better version of who we thought we were. This can be the perfect time to rebuild an identity that you really value, not one shaped by what you do for a living or what people expect of you. This is your chance to re-define *who* you are, what you believe in and stand for, to become a more confident person with a deeper love, stronger values and an appreciation for what really matters in life.

CHAPTER 12

J

... is for 'Joining a group'

Five years ago as I prepared for the birth of my first child, I underestimated the enormity of how my lifestyle would change. I was working 50-plus-hour weeks in the corporate environment and helping out in the family business on weekends. I was also part of a local running group, an active gym member and had a full social life that involved going out for regular dinners, to new bar openings and on spontaneous shopping expeditions. My busy lifestyle entitled me to endless interaction and stimulation with different people from all walks of life. It made the weeks really enjoyable and interesting and I was inspired as a person by the many people I encountered.

Yet it didn't take long for everything to turn on its head. After giving birth I found myself cooped up at home seven days a week, 24 hours a day, sometimes not talking to anybody. I did not have friends or relatives who had children and maternity leave at the same time as I did, so I didn't even have someone I could have a coffee and a laugh with to break up the day. My partner worked weekends as well, so for me every day just blended into the next.

I couldn't resume the same social life as I had before because the circumstances were different. For starters, I was out of the workforce and no longer included in the weekly lunches or monthly drinks anymore. The times for the running group didn't suit feed, bath and sleep routines, and I was far from entering the gym. It was also difficult to go out with friends for dinner or shopping because our schedules no longer meshed and early on I found it difficult to part with my baby.

The days are pretty long and monotonous when you are constantly on your own. Fortunately, I had mothers' group to look forward to. Mothers' group is designed to prepare new mums for the dramatic weeks to come. To me, it felt more like a lifeline and a way to normalise what all new parents go through. Being part of this group, like being part of any group, gave me the chance to make friends, establish relationships, and gain a greater sense of control over a part of my life.

When you have given birth and are ready to go home, the hospital will normally put you in touch with a Maternal or Early Childhood Health Centre in your neighbourhood. This is where you are likely to take your baby to be weighed, measured and reviewed by nurses qualified in child and family health. As a first-time mum, you will also be registered on a list with other mothers who live in the area and who have also given birth recently. When there are approximately six to twelve mums listed, the centre will start a term of weekly meetings hosted by a midwife.

'I've met a few mums who baulk at the corny idea of being introduced to strangers who live in your area who all happen to have had a baby around the same. You'll be surprised how lonely it can be at times and how a weekly coffee with other mums going through the exact same thing at the same time can actually be a refreshing break to the routine.'

— Gloria (33), mum to Helen (three)

During each weekly mothers' group meeting, the nurse will discuss a topic such as post-natal depression, sleeping and feeding patterns, sex and intimacy after birth, first aid, settling techniques, and other relevant subjects. Mothers have the opportunity to learn, ask questions, compare notes, participate in discussion and just generally debrief about their experiences. The sessions are usually followed by a coffee and a chat. After the term finishes, the mums can decide if they want to resume meeting up in their own environments and pursue friendships.

'When I walked into the room and met the other mums for the first time, I was judgmental and decided that they weren't really my "type". Yet strip away the dress sense, nationalities, professions and we were all the same: intelligent, first-time mums who wanted to enjoy the motherhood experience and break up the boredom for sanity's sake. It's been over four years and we are still a tight pack, having bonded over our own personal trials and tribulations. Even though we all have our own friends as well, it is pretty clear we will forever have this "group" with which to vent and enjoy a coffee or dinner.'

— Michelle (38), mum to Jonathon (four) and Georgie (one)

This group environment worked out well for me, as it has for many others. It provides an opportunity to form an instant group and possible friendships with new mothers who not only live locally, but are also going through the same stage of motherhood. So you can discuss issues you can all relate to and swap notes on anything from growth spurts, weight-loss tips and great new activities, to products and places to try with baby.

'I never expected to love being part of a mums' group as much as I have. It just worked out that we all got along like we'd known each other forever. We have a pretty tight bond and catch up with the kids weekly, as couples monthly and even indulge in girl-only pampering weekends once a year.'

— Peta (31), mum to Jodie (two)

It is not just a great release for the mums. If you are lucky enough to form a bond and continue a relationship, the children grow up with an instant network of friends. They learn to interact with other children and can be entertained by each other while you enjoy a coffee and chat.

'Our children have been spending time with one another regularly since they were born. They are now eight years old. Not only do all the kids get along and share a beautiful, familiar bond, it is so emotional and lovely to host joint birthday parties and watch the babies grow into independent, gorgeous children.

Sure, I've been given the opportunity to meet other mums in the area, but it is also lovely to know that my child has some neighbourhood friends who are there for her too.'

— Milla (36), mum to Lisa (eight), Riley (five) and Jasper (one)

Yet not everyone feels the need to be a part of this formal network. You might be surrounded by friends and relatives with their own children. Perhaps they live nearby and are available for regular interaction and consultation, so you know you have the support you need at any time.

Alternatively, you might be reluctant or too shy to join a group and prefer to go about things on your own. But if you are missing out on regular contact and stimulation from other mothers just like you and feeling isolated because you don't have many friends around, then a mothers' group can be like a social, group therapy session, able to guide you through concerns and difficult moments.

'I didn't genuinely get along with all the girls in the group and found the circle sort of fizzled after about three months. However, there was one mum there who was just like me. We had so much in common and continued to catch up at least once a week and speak on the phone daily. We have been best of friends for six years, and two kids later we continue to support each other for the different ups and downs we all go through. Our families even holiday together. While the whole "mothers' group" didn't work out, it has been so great having her in my life and I really appreciate the friendship we have developed.'

— Melissa (35), mum to Christine (six) and George (one)

Mothers' groups aren't for everyone. Sometimes, there is a struggle to find enough common ground to keep seeing each other socially. And that's life. You can't get along with everyone. If you did not fit in with the personalities in the mothers' group you were assigned to, you can either chat to your Maternal Centre about switching over to another local group or you can contact other independent bodies that run alternative groups for mothers in your community.

'Mums' group was not for me. I had such good intentions, but after a few catch-ups it was pretty clear I did not fit in. We had very different backgrounds, personalities and interests and couldn't find enough common ground with which to form a friendship.'

— Kimberley (28), mum to Joy (one)

'I am not interested in hearing about how many times your kids pooped, or tell you about how many times mine vomited. I can't think of anything more boring.'

— Karen (36), mum to Jeorja (three) and André (one)

Perhaps you have enough baby talk in your own life and the thought of spending more time with others and hearing their baby talk and disgusting number two stories is the most uninteresting thing you can think of. While you relish the idea of escaping from the mundane routine for a few hours a week, your interests and personality might be better suited elsewhere.

Your needs can also change. A mothers' group might be just what you need for the first three months, but thereafter you might want to look for another group to participate in. Perhaps you are considering going back to work and want to spend more time networking with other business professionals. Or you might want to get more physically active and prefer the company and motivation a group sports session provides. Or you might be considering a new hobby and want to mix more with others who share your passion.

'I'm a shy person by nature, but at the time we had relocated to a different state and I did not have anyone I knew. I realised that I was going to have to make the effort to meet others, otherwise I would be left pretty isolated and forced to cling onto only my partner for that constant adult interaction. I've always been into sports, so I thought it would be worthwhile joining a basketball team.

I was nervous in the beginning, but after the first couple of weeks, things flowed from there and it ended up being a great break to the week. Plus, it was great because there were other mums in the team as well. I had to push myself to get out there in the beginning, but I did manage to widen my circle and get fit in the process.'

— Tracey (32), mum to Ross (two)

It's amazing what groups and resources are available to assist you in your transition period. Just opening the local paper or doing a quick internet search can introduce you to hundreds of different groups you could participate in. Business groups, sporting groups, support groups, hobby groups, mothers' groups, playgroups, book groups, theatre groups, cooking groups, and so on are all available and offer great benefits for a new mother. It is just a matter of considering what your mind and body are craving and locating a group that will address your needs.

Ten benefits of joining a group

1. You temporarily run away from the role of 'mum'.
2. A group can motivate you to learn something new.
3. It's an opportunity to interact with different members of society.
4. You can get inspired by a new environment/topic/people.
5. You can continue to evolve your identity as a woman and an individual.
6. It pushes you out of your comfort zone.
7. It re-invigorates your mindset, attitude and routine.
8. It's a way to start developing the new you.
9. You can feel part of a team again.
10. It's a way to nurture and respect your interests, passions and needs.

The thought of participating in a group may sound daunting, especially if you are uncomfortable in new environments or timid when it comes to making new friends. But once you get to know everyone and they get to know you, your participation and contribution become more recognised. As group members, you can inspire one another to personally develop and achieve something — either for yourselves or as a group. This also leads to a sense of accomplishment and satisfaction.

Ten ways to make joining a group easier

If you are very shy and nervous about joining a group, or struggle to find the motivation to try new things, there are a few ways to make the process easier.

1. Find a group that you genuinely have an interest in or passion for — you will be more motivated to be involved.

2. Do some research — ask others if they can recommend a group. That way you know in advance if that sporting/mothers'/networking, etc., group is friendly, welcoming and conducted in a way that suits your style.

3. Join with a friend — that way you start with a support partner.

4. Ask a contact to introduce you on your behalf — this is helpful if you know someone who is already acquainted with a group you would like to participate in.

5. Ask questions, compliment and be pleasant to others in the group, while being natural — most people will feel flattered and will welcome your company.

6. Take small steps — aim to have a conversation with just one new person in the group each week. Before long you will have familiarised yourself with everyone.

7. Be a great listener — remember a fact about the different group members and ask them about it in a conversation at a subsequent meeting. This will give you an excuse to converse and continue a relationship.

8. Consider online groups — these can be easier to join because you can keep a sense of anonymity as you get to know other participants. Then, as you feel more comfortable, you can consider meeting up in person.

HELLO
my name is

9. Ask in advance how new members are introduced to a group of interest — this way you might find out that everyone is new and they have some introductory activities, or you will be appointed a partner who can guide you for a few weeks. By knowing what to expect you will feel more confident about how you can fit in.

10. Don't put unnecessary pressure on yourself — just enjoy the process and what you could learn. Don't expect to make new best friends in this group. Instead, see it for what it is, which is a way to explore an activity and interact with different people to develop your personal interests.

CHAPTER 13

... is for 'Keeping up appearances'

'Before kids you would always find me in sexy jeans and a stylish top with the latest accessories. My hair smelt great and I looked healthy and glowing. Fast forward to after kids and I would most likely be found in the mum uniform. You might have it yourself. It consists of no make-up, no perfume, hair (that feels like cardboard) pulled back in a ponytail, wearing leggings or tracksuit pants and an old t-shirt that nobody should wear in public.

Why should I bother when I am too busy feeding, cooking or slumped on the couch from utter exhaustion?

I know my husband would never expect me to or love me less for not wearing heels and a designer dress, but my change in appearance said something. It said I don't care about how I present myself any more. I am no longer a priority and I don't take pride in how I look. I am too tired to make an effort.

Six months later, I can still be found in leggings and a t-shirt ... But I get my nails done, my hair coloured and I'm always wearing perfume. I do these things for me and nobody else. They make me feel good about myself. If I feel good about myself I know I can achieve great things.

I recommend you get out of the mum uniform or, at the very least, bring back some of your personality to your styling. You will feel more like your sexy, bright, happy self, rather than a frumpy, sloppy and made to sit on the floor mama, picking mashed banana off the carpet.'

— Janet (30), mum to Chloe (six months)

This chapter is about respecting your appearance the way you did before you had a baby and about genuinely believing that you still matter. This chapter is not about trying to look like a Stepford wife or celebrity mum, about compromising all your other commitments to make yourself look like you just stepped out of a fashion catalogue, or about relying purely on looks to make yourself feel good.

You are not 'just' a mum or someone who should live and breathe the stereotypical mum uniform. You are a woman who deserves to feel healthy, happy, confident and gorgeous within her own skin. And sometimes it takes a little primping and polishing to create and maintain that feel-good attitude. That's what this chapter is about: valuing the fact that, despite having a baby who takes up so much time and energy, you still deserve to look and feel great about yourself, for yourself. You should continue to make that effort to maintain a part of your pre-baby identity and image.

Do you remember the effort you went to pre-baby to make yourself look gorgeous, if for no one but yourself? You more than likely showered regularly, slapped on some fake tan, plucked your eyebrows, shaved your legs, blowdried your hair, had regular waxing appointments, used cleansers and moisturisers, and even wore make-up.

'I caught myself thinking the other day, as I welcomed my husband home, how times had changed since we had kids. I remember I used to "tidy myself up" before he would arrive home by putting on a slick of gloss and a spray of perfume. I wanted to look fresh. It made me feel good about myself. And if I felt good he'd pick up the vibe and we'd welcome each other with a very raunchy kiss that set the tone for the night.

Today, I'm unwashed, wearing a faded tracksuit, grubby slippers, hair tied back, no make-up or perfume on and I just look exhausted. Needless to say, the raunchy kiss is replaced with a quick peck. It's not that my husband doesn't find me attractive. *I* didn't feel attractive, confident or radiating any glow. And because of how I was feeling about myself, I didn't want to get too intimate with him. And that attitude also set the tone for the night.'

— Marissa (37), mum to Tailer (three) and Emily (one)

Surveys suggest that the majority of mums have a more negative perspective on their appearance after baby than they did before. And it doesn't help that there is seemingly less time and energy to actually do something about it after giving birth. It's completely normal at this point in time to devote more time to caring for baby than for oneself. For obvious reasons, a mum will neglect herself entirely in the beginning, forgetting to eat, sleep and do anything that even remotely resembles a beauty and grooming routine.

'I used to exfoliate, cleanse and put a mask on my face weekly. Now I only do it when it looks like my face is starting to rot ... It's bitter sweet that our babies once gave us a gorgeous pregnancy glow, movie star locks and steel-hard nails for nine months, only to take it away faster than you can say "epidural".'

— Stephanie (41), mum to Baxter (eleven) and Joey (eight)

We give so much love and time to our children that we ignore the stretch marks, the uneven breasts, wider hips, excess pregnancy weight, sagging skin or grey hairs and vow to deal with our cellulite, unnecessary facial hair, dull skin and dark roots another time. Who worries about this sort of superficial stuff when we have an intoxicating little miracle to wake up to, dote on and devote our lives to?

It is time for a reality check. If you are still thinking like this you obviously haven't weighed yourself, tried on your pre-baby jeans, freaked out over a recent wedding invitation or bumped into an old friend or work colleague who is also a mum but who looks stunning. Alas, the time will come when you will have to make the decision to resume making an effort with your appearance or learn to absolutely accept and adore the wobbly, hairy, unkempt and smelly new you ... for a very long time.

If this idea seems a little harder to swallow than actually making the effort, don't stress. A new improvised maintenance routine will get you out of the mummy rut and make the thought of looking after yourself easy, desirable and one of the best things you can do for you and your baby to promote a healthy mind, body and attitude. And looking after your appearance can fit in with looking after baby.

Making an effort to look good is not just so that other people find you attractive. It is so that you feel good about yourself. When you feel good about yourself, you have a more positive self-esteem, confidence and exude a bit of spunk. As a result, the people around you will genuinely enjoy being around your energy. Then you continue to feel good and carry that attitude through the day. The good vibes just keep on coming.

Perhaps you think, 'Why should I bother?', 'Who has the time?', 'I spend the day changing nappies/singing nursery rhymes/washing clothes and cleaning vomit' or 'Nobody sees me anyway'. This is your negative inner voice saying you are no longer a priority and there are other things that matter more. If you think like this for too long you will wake up one day, look in the mirror and not recognise the face staring back. Just imagine: roots showing against brassy hair colour; overgrown, shapeless eyebrows;

twenty-year-old unshapely jeans; underwear fit for a grandmother, unwaxed top lip and not a push-up bra in sight. Don't let this happen to you!

You used to bother, make the time and, most of all, care. It was part of your personality and identity and made you feel 'like yourself'. Sure, you have a child now who will no doubt take up a lot of your time, but it doesn't mean that your energy and effort only goes to the child. You are important too and should make the effort to address your needs to look and feel good about yourself.

'My mother said to me, "So long as I have lipstick on, I don't care what the house looks like." What she meant was, it's more important for the woman to look good and feel good than it is to get the housework done. Some people might be a little shocked at this and think she is lazy, but she is getting her priorities right. It is more important for her to feel fabulous.'

— Tracy (38), mum to Hannah (four) and Bridget (two)

When you arrive home from the hospital, it won't take you long to realise that what you used to do to rejuvenate your appearance isn't quite so convenient now. But that doesn't mean you throw in the towel and accept a less than glamorous version of yourself. You improvise.

'After about two months of slumming it, I got myself into a new habit. Every Thursday night after I put the baby to sleep, I would lock myself in the bathroom. I'd bathe, moisturise, pluck, put on some fake tan and style my hair. I felt like a new woman and would enter the weekend feeling motivated and wanting to get out there with civilisation. If I really had the energy I'd also pop into a nearby shopping complex and buy new knickers, lipstick or earrings. Nothing extravagant or too expensive. Just something to freshen up my appearance.'

— Athena (31), mum to Lucia (two)

Depending on your grooming habits before baby, some things might need to be compromised, albeit temporarily. Regular spray tans, three-hour gym sessions and expensive lash extensions might be difficult to afford or schedule if you don't have someone to babysit or the extra funds available if you have dropped an income. However, there is still so much you can do.

'I used to get my nails done fortnightly but now I cut, polish and file them myself. I used to have my hair treated monthly, but now my girlfriend comes around and does it for me — out of the box, mind you. But I still get my eyebrows done professionally and often. It's a little treat, just for me.'

— Janine (38), mum to Donovan (four) and Maxine (one)

'When my baby was having her morning nap I could get out of bed and catch up with housework, paperwork and anything else I was behind in. Instead I would sleep an extra half hour, have a hot bubble bath, "put my face on", brush my hair and enjoy my morning coffee. I did this every day for about the first six weeks. This helped my body recover and got me into a new beauty habit early on. Because of this, I was feeling good, instead of sleep deprived and haggard, when my baby woke for a feed. It really gave me an energetic and positive mind set for the day.'

— Skye (33), mum to Mel (two)

Regular showers, a daily spray of your favourite perfume, a quick slick of the glossiest lipstick, the occasional hair treatment and the odd pedicure will go a long way to making you feel clean and refreshed. And you don't need to spend a fortune. There are hundreds of do-it-yourself solutions, neighbourhood specials and friends who can assist.

'When I was working, I used to have $200 haircuts, but now that I was home and we were relying on one income, I just couldn't justify them any more. Instead of giving up, I looked for coupons or discount vouchers for all my beauty treatments or alternated between giving myself a treatment and getting something done professionally, so I didn't blow the household budget. This way I didn't feel at all guilty and still looked and felt wonderful.'

— Nita (33), mum to Dimitri (four) and Luke (two)

Previously it took you 45 minutes to get ready for the day, now you have a ten-minute window before you need to feed, settle or burp. If you struggle to find the time you had before, don't be deterred. Instead, do one or two of the things that always used to be part of your routine and made you feel a million dollars.

Have a quick shower and spray on your favourite perfume. Style your hair and put on your lipstick. Put on some face cream and a sparkly pair of earrings. We all have things that instantly boost our esteem and make us feel nice, clean and pretty. Identify that one thing and make it part of your routine every day, the way you prioritise brushing your teeth. Do it whether you are going out, staying home, expecting company or not. Do it for you. Do it because you used to do it for you and it is part of who you are.

'Whenever my mum would come over she would practically chase me around the room until she'd brushed my hair and put some lipstick on me. In her words that's what made her feel "human again" and motivated her for the day. She just wanted the same for me. Foundation and a little mascara is more my thing, but I totally understood what her intentions were.'

— Katerina (36), mum to Mary (four) and Michael (three)

'My best friend always looked good before having her baby. Even if she was wearing a tracksuit, you can be sure she had clean, glossy hair, smelt divine and wore her signature Tiffany's bracelet. She always had this glow about her.

When she had a baby she was so hormonal and out of sorts she just could not find the motivation to even shower. This was not her. Making an effort to look fresh and fashionable was part of who she was. I had to step in and basically force her to shower every day and fix herself up. After a week of this she had made it part of her routine to start off by making herself up — even a little. Not because she wanted to look like a star but because she wanted to feel like one. This way, she was herself again. She had a better self-esteem, felt happy, glowing, confident and ready for the day.'

— Thelma (31), mum to Diana (three)

If you feel guilty about doing this for you, do it for your child. Set an example. You want your child to grow up to respect themselves. You would demand that they took the time and made the effort to feel good. You would expect them to prioritise themselves because they are worth it. You don't want your child to ever neglect themselves, so this is your chance to be their role model.

'Whenever I style my hair out, or wear something other than my walking gear, my three-year-old daughter will say to me, "You look pretty, Mummy." It's so sweet.

I'm always telling her how important it is to keep clean, the benefits of exercise, brushing teeth, massages and how these things are good for us and make our bodies work better. And it's true.

Looking after ourselves shows respect for our bodies. I want her to see that I make the effort so that she does too. I want her to take pride in her appearance, respect herself and care for her mind and body so she feels good about herself always. There is nothing wrong with that. I'm not telling her she has to look like a supermodel to be valued. I'm telling her it is healthy to take pride in herself.'

— Natarsha (33), mum to Adele (three)

Five ways to make looking after yourself easier and more affordable

1. Start the day by doing one thing each morning that makes you feel good about yourself.
2. Don't leave the house without doing something you used to pre-baby, such as putting on lipstick or perfume.
3. Throw out any unfashionable, unflattering, stained clothes and underwear.
4. Schedule a regular do-it-yourself beauty and pampering night.
5. Look for discount vouchers or coupons for beauty treatments.

Five reasons you should take pride in your appearance

1. To set an example for your child to love and respect her own body.
2. To feel more confident in yourself and to have a more positive self-esteem.
3. To motivate you on your journey to do amazing things as a mother and a woman.
4. To express your identity and personality as an individual.
5. To demonstrate that you still matter.

CHAPTER 14

... is for 'Love, sex and romance'

'I noticed that I would give all my love, time, affection and nurturing to my baby all day. By the time my husband and I would get into bed there was just nothing left for me to give. All the energy I used to have for him was now being given to my child. And I got so much love back from my baby that sex, love and intimacy from my partner weren't my priority anymore. I've heard it's a normal feeling and reaction, but I don't recommend it for the long term.'

— Charlotte (26), mum to Sienna (one)

Love, sex and romance are the three key things you once shared with your partner that are most likely to cop the biggest beating as a result of having a child. It might be long term or short term. Either way, it is very common for couples to go through a transition period in these three areas, as they get accustomed to the change in dynamics, routine, emotions and needs.

It should really come as no surprise. So much has changed. Once upon a time you only had eyes, time, money and energy for each other. You were his number one, and he, yours. You might have lavished gifts on one another, enjoyed unspoiled couple time, opened the door naked occasionally, been sent beautiful flowers, shared dirty emails, spent the day in bed, flirted and really cherished having each other. It feels like a lifetime ago. Now there is so much more in your life that you did not have to deal with before.

You are sleep deprived, battling body image issues, drained from being at someone's beck and call all day, hungry, unkempt and seriously hormonal. Your partner might not be in a better position either. He might have more to worry about as he feels the pressure of being the provider, his sleep is also disturbed, he has more to do around the home and is likely to come home after a full-on day at work only to be handed a screaming child before he has time to take his shoes off. And he has no chance of any sympathy from you.

It's unlikely either of you can be bothered shaving, let alone writing love letters, arranging romantic weekends, sending flowers or offering each other sensual oil massages. Get real. In the beginning, all you wish for is a full night's sleep, food in the pantry, a clean house, the occasional shower and a quiet, contented baby. Everything you once desired isn't quite that desirable right now.

'Before kids, and even during pregnancy actually, my sex drive was out of control — perhaps even higher than my husband's. Any position, anytime and anywhere and I was up for it. *But*, post baby I would baulk at the idea of sex. Are you kidding? I was too tired, stressed and so not in the mood. How can you be in the mood for sex and intimacy after you have been up all night, you have mastitis and stitches to deal with, other kids to chase after and just feel physically and mentally drained. It took months before we got to that stage again.'

— Melanie (42), mum to Thomai (eleven) and Brittany (seven)

But just because it is easy to understand how and why love, sex and romance can go awry, that doesn't mean you should forget about these three important things you both once prioritised. After all, the love, sex and romance you once shared with your partner are the reason for your own little miracle who now stares back at you with unconditional love. That love, sex and romance also nurtured an intimacy between you and created some heartwarming memories. They are what keep your chemistry, passion and connection alive.

If you want all of this back in your life then it will take some effort from both sides. More effort than was required previously. It's different now, because there are lots of little changes taking place in your relationship that collectively influence things overall.

'For the past six years my partner and I traditionally held hands while we were driving somewhere. It is just a nice intimate thing we have always done. When our child was getting older and more alert he would absolutely crack it if we were holding hands. He did not want to share his mum. Well, sorry to say, but we caved in and stopped holding hands, purely to put a stop to the screaming and whinging. He was too young for us to explain why we did it, and it was easier to just give in. It might not sound like a big deal to you, but for me it was just a nice, sweet moment my partner and I have always shared and another romantic part of us that slipped away.'

— Jill (36), mum to Mitchell (four) and Lucy (one)

A simple thing like holding hands is now too hard because someone needs to push the pram. Talking to each other over a hot meal is a challenge because the baby is restless, hungry or wet. Showing off some attractive lingerie is impossible as you now live in maternity bras, breast pads or a machine fit to milk a farm. Spontaneity is also somewhat diminished. You can't just go out, have sex in the kitchen, cuddle whenever the mood arises or even finish a conversation with your partner because you have feed time, bath time, sleep time and play time to coordinate first.

'Yes, our sex life was interrupted. We would be in the swing of things, in my favourite position, with me on top and having a pretty good time, then my breasts would start leaking drops of milk. It took a minute before the let-down came and I was squirting my husband's face and chest with warm breast milk — with full force, let me tell you. Poor guy barely had a chance to come up for air. I am a size E and I had enough milk to feed half the starving kids in Africa. Lucky he didn't drown.

Tell me, how do you continue doing it after that that? I couldn't stop laughing hysterically. Going forward I had to have sex while wearing my maternity bra, with breastfeeding pads. It was just too messy otherwise. Yeah, took the sexiness out of it a little. But what do you do?'

— Georgina (38), mum to Ross (seven) and Natasha (five)

It all sounds very scary doesn't it? You think for a moment you will never again get to put the 'L' back into 'love', experience impulsive hot sex or feel romanced and treasured the way you once were. But you will and it can be as fulfilling and frequent as you resolve to make it. The choice is yours. You can give up, give in or make the effort to fit love, sex and romance into your daily life and genuinely enjoy yourself, your partner and your relationship in the process.

'If my husband wants to turn me on for sex all he has to do now is the housework, without asking. Best foreplay ever. Gets me every time.'

— Jean (36), mum to Michael and Morris (four)

You know, there are actually many mums out there who are experiencing a love and sex life like never before and have found different ways to keep the romance alive. Some would even argue (shock horror!) that it is actually better after baby because you have a stronger connection, greater respect for your body and deeper love for the partner who gave you the world.

This is what you can learn from these women to promote love, sex and romance in your life:

- Resolve to make the effort.
- Communicate.
- Start a new habit.
- Do something that makes you feel sexy.
- Just have fun.
- Change your mindset and look forward to it.

Make the effort

Having a healthy relationship with all the trimmings is not hard; it just requires effort from both parties. You do have to work at having love, sex and romance in your life, but the rewards are worth it. Think about what you did to have these things in your life before.

Maybe you went out for dinner weekly, made a big deal out of anniversaries, bought each other random gifts, complimented each other, talked a lot, had breakfast in bed on Sundays, Friday night sex night, helped each other do things or shared a common hobby or sport. For obvious reasons, these little things can be forgotten very quickly. Once you recognise where the love, sex and romance have withered, try to restart what is possible and substitute the rest with new ways to show your love.

You can call your partner at work when the baby is sleeping, to catch up on life. You can turn the TV off every Tuesday night at 7.30 to just hang out with no distractions.

Replace your Friday night boozy sex tradition with a Sunday afternoon sex tradition while the baby naps. Lock in a babysitter for every second Saturday so you go out together, just the two of you. Make a conscious effort to say something positive, complimentary or supportive to each other on a daily basis. The only things stopping you are excuses, neglect and not placing sex, love and romance on your priority list.

'My parents' marriage broke down after all three of their kids had left the house and I blame the breakdown partly on the fact that they did not invest in their relationship as a man and a woman should. My parents neglected each other while they were raising their three kids and once we were off their hands they did not know each other any more, had no common interests and had developed into two totally different people.

I'm not going to fall into that trap. We are going to keep our chemistry alive at least two nights a week, by dressing up for each other instead of living in weathered tracksuits, flirting, laughing, talking and genuinely enjoying each other's company the way we always have; the way it is too difficult to do when you are stuck inside a messy home, with chores staring at you, the pillow beckoning you to sleep and the baby demanding a feed, clean nappy or entertainment.

After my baby was born I jumped into a habit most people only dream of. I got a babysitter two nights a week, so that my husband and I could go out as a couple. This meant that two nights a week, while our baby was in safe hands, we could let our hair down and enjoy quality time together, away from the routine and madness at home and just be ourselves — not a mum and a dad.

Two nights a week we get to invest time into our relationship and reconnect. My husband I spend time talking about work, issues, dreams, aspirations and what we are going to achieve as a family. The support and quality time is invaluable as we come home relaxed, inspired for the future, connected as a couple and genuinely in the mood to have sex. Short-term and long-term benefits all round.

It is important to me that my husband and I have a connection away from our child. It has been fourteen months now and we are still doing it.'

— Mei-Lin (34), mum to Evelyn (fourteen months)

Communicate

You and your partner might have always communicated well in the past and had all the time in the world to talk, listen and resolve issues. These days, you're lucky if you have a daily conversation that goes for twenty minutes thanks to all the distractions. Then, when the baby is in bed for the night, you just want to rest and zone out.

You don't always have the energy to talk about what is truly on your mind. You gradually bottle everything up and eventually explode over a minor issue, like him not putting the milk away. You find yourself yelling, 'I had an awful day today cleaning up vomit, I'm still upset that you didn't tell me you are going out with the boys tomorrow and you haven't even noticed my new hair style!' when what you mean to say is, 'I'm feeling a bit depressed and neglected and I think it would be great if we did something nice, just us, this weekend. I need a bit of a break from this routine.'

We can't always read each other's mind, so it helps if you share concerns without the yelling, screaming and accusations that will only fuel unconstructive arguments. When something is on your mind, find the right time to talk it out so that the other half knows what is going on in your head and can be there to offer support, encouragement and acknowledgement. Otherwise, issues can build up but you're too absorbed in daily life to pay attention to the subtle cues.

'Sometimes my husband will come home from work and zone out in front of the TV or computer for hours then when we go to bed he wants me to roll over and have sex.

I know he is tired as well, but I am a woman, not a machine, and I still want to feel loved and desired. We have spoken about it and he knows I need foreplay in the form of attention, some flirting and general acknowledgement way before we go anywhere near the bedroom.

Fortunately, we communicate well with each other and I tell him straight out that he still needs to work on me. Just because we have been together for a while and have kids, doesn't mean he should take me for granted. It's good that we can talk about things.

It took him a while but he finally admitted that sometimes he also feels neglected by me, because I am too preoccupied to pay him the attention I used to. I have since changed a few things. I call him during his lunch break, when the baby is sleeping, and spend twenty minutes just talking. I realised we never speak for twenty minutes without being interrupted at home. We were lucky if we used to get through the basic day-to-day dialogue before something interrupted us.

I also try to do one small, nice thing for him every other day. Like making him a coffee unexpectedly, buying his favourite bar of chocolate and not swearing at him too much when he snores like an animal at two in the morning when I am yet to fall asleep. I show him I still care.'

— Nikki (28), mum to Paige (seven) and George (four)

Start a new habit

Now that you are a mum, the chances are that many of your old habits are just a distant memory. Going forward, you can either take each day as it comes and be reactive to everything you are faced with, or become proactive in starting new habits that will provide you with more control over your love life. It takes 30 days to start a new habit, so in less than a month love, sex and romance will fit into your daily life, naturally.

To make it easier to start, just choose one new habit that you know will lead to a more fulfilling love life. Once you have that habit down pat, look at introducing a new one. You might want to shower together every Thursday night, cook a meal together every Sunday afternoon or give each other a massage or foot rubs every Monday. Just select something you would both enjoy and resolve to make it a priority for that moment.

'The spicy nights tend to fade after kids and long days at work. However, my partner and I actively work at our love life. If anyone is looking for a little inspiration, this is what I would suggest:

Wine and sex night. It may not sound romantic and spontaneous, but it keeps your love life going; my husband can't wait to get home on Wednesday nights.

Go and buy yourself some matching lingerie. When the kids are in bed, put on some heels and model your new underwear for your hubby. Buy him some so he can do the same, minus the heels.

Date night in. No TV, just dinner, wine and your favourite CDs.

Hotel night, just because. It is more romantic when it is not for a special occasion.

Friday night beer 'n' bath. Spend Friday nights drinking beer in the bath together with your favourite takeaway. Great way to unwind from a busy week and it sets the tone for a great weekend. Your hubby will love it, he gets to drink beer, check out his wife naked, and eat pizza.'

— Virginia (40), mum to Ella (four) and Edward (two)

Do something that makes you feel sexy

When you feel sexy, you also feel more confident and empowered. You radiate a vibe that your other half will sense and will want to get close to. You might feel sexy when you have slapped on fake tan, blowdried your hair or are wearing Coco Chanel perfume. The point is you have done something to make you feel like a natural woman, rather than a mum who has been building sandcastles all day.

'There is no way I am going to wear my sexy, racy, lacy (and only matching) lingerie that promises the wearer sex, if I have not been waxed. I struggle to look at myself in the mirror let alone feel confident with my sexual prowess if I am as hairy and *au naturel* as a '60s hippy. Nope. Just can't do it. My husband is willing and able even if I haven't showered for two weeks (not that I have left it that long), but I need to sometimes feel sexy just for me and my self-esteem. When I make the effort to wax, primp and polish, I feel hot, more confident and I bring that attitude into the bedroom.'

— Vanessa (36), mum to Verity and Zara (four)

Just have fun

Mortgages, school options, bills, nappy rashes, appraisals, doctor's appointments, annoying mothers-in-law and so much more make life very serious at times. Sometimes, we need to take a leaf out of our children's books and start enjoying the simple things in life more. As they say, 'Don't sweat the small stuff.' Laugh and joke with each other to nurture your sense of humour. As a result, you'll feel lighter, happier and will actually enjoy life and each other so much more.

'My husband took me by surprise one day. He asked me to wear this surprisingly sexy black, lacy maternity bra while we were having sex and wanted me to "pop open" the flaps mid way. I know it's funny, but at least we were being innovative and making the most of our new circumstances. I told some of my friends, and though they had a good chuckle at my expense, they ended up surprising their hubbies as well.

Just because you are a mum, you can't take everything too seriously. It's nice to still be able to have fun in the bedroom and just enjoy the moment, even if it is a little different to how it used to be.'

— Estherina (37), mum to Luthia (nine), Michaela (five) and Andres (two)

Change your mindset and actually look forward to it

Don't view having sex, romancing each other and demonstrating your love as another job you have to tick off your list or brace yourself for. See it as a way to bond, reconnect, release some steam and reclaim a moment that belongs to just the two of you.

Start thinking sexy, romantic thoughts from the beginning of the day. Remember things you used to do as a couple that you really took pleasure from. Think about why you love him. Value why he is in your life and show him or tell him what he means to you.

Just because you are a mother now that doesn't mean you don't need or benefit from intimacy. Look forward to being intimate with your partner, either physically or emotionally, and visualise how nice it feels when you have that comfort. You will find you will then make time for it in your day.

It is too easy to forget how nice it feels to be close to someone when you don't experience it too often. It's up to you to make the effort to remember and prioritise it as something you want in your day and life.

CHAPTER 15

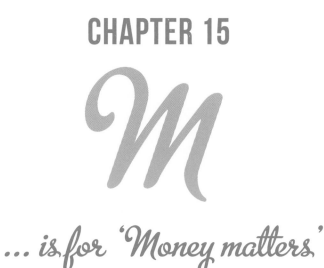

... is for 'Money matters'

'I am willing to sacrifice some non-essentials for the luxury of being able to be there for my baby as he laughs for the first time, walks for the first time and says my name for the first time. This is just a phase that addresses my current priorities. I would rather be home with my baby than working to afford a brand new car.'

— Carmella (33), mum to Robert (nine months)

'I miss working and having the extra cash but my partner and I made the decision to sacrifice certain things for the sake of one of us being there for the children until they get to school age. I would love the extra money but it's going to have to wait until I go back to work.'

— Robyn (44), mum to Courtney (three) and Alexia (eleven months)

Parenting resources are quick to tell you how to feed the baby, set a routine, handle colic and a child that won't sleep, but forget to explain how to budget, accommodate a reduced income and actually cope with the dramatic change. Some families might not be affected by financial restraints after having a child. Perhaps they set themselves up beforehand, their partners earn more than enough or they simply have plenty of money. Others can happily live with the basics in life or will resume work immediately.

However, a vast percentage of families having children are not fully financially prepared. Most will feel the pinch and be forced to adjust to new spending habits — reluctantly. This is especially true if you take an unpaid leave of absence from work to be a stay-at-home mum, thereby reducing the money coming into the household just as expenses naturally rise.

It can also be a major psychological adjustment for the woman if she has given up work to be at home full time. Pre-baby, many stay-at-home mums earned a wage and had control over how it was spent, but now they most likely have no wage to earn or spend. There are new restrictions and a loss of financial independence to deal with.

'I know that we are a family and it is "our" money and I am still "working". Yet it took me a while to adjust to having less money. After six months I picked up one shift a week at work, just so I could reclaim some play money. It's hard to go without when you are so used to buying and spending as you please for so long.'

— Roberta (34), mum to Kelly (three) and Andrew (one)

'I guess I felt like I was still working, because I was. Taking care of the baby and the household was more demanding than any job I had. Except in this role, unfortunately, you don't automatically get a salary deposited into your account on a monthly basis, which is a bit disappointing.'

— Calista (29), mum to Cameron (two)

If you are like me (and thousands of others), you enjoy the freedom and frivolity of spending money. It's a great pastime to go out for lunch, get hair and nails done, buy your family treats for no particular reason and pay someone else to do your ironing.

'There is no way I can do this forever. I miss the clothes, I miss the holidays, I miss the splurges. I don't like having to think twice about taking the kids out for lunch, or buying a toy on impulse.'

— Paige (30), mum to Melinda and Coral (one)

In society today, we have grown accustomed to having what we want, when we want it. Some of us charge the credit card; others work hard. Either way, we have everything at our disposal and haven't been forced to live without. Like many other Gen X and Y mums, this attitude and spending habit is what I am accustomed to. Yet, as is the case for many other families, I also recognise that it takes two incomes to afford the mortgage and life we want. It is a big deal for this generation to sacrifice and live with less.

'I am not a frivolous or extravagant spender, nor am I a brand snob. I am just used to doing and buying stuff for myself and my family without a second thought, because I have always worked to afford these things. I have never unrealistically spent beyond my means or employed a house cleaner and I almost always cook from scratch. I am just a regular, hard-working, independent, middle-class woman ... who had a baby.'

— Lola (36), mum to Ollie (seven) and Rebecca (four)

I struggled to accept the new spending restraints placed upon me when I stopped work. Firstly, there was no more money coming into my bank account. Secondly, the guilt escalated at the thought of continuing to enjoy expensive haircuts and nail appointments; and thirdly, I was absolutely robbed of the financial independence that I had rightfully earned.

'My husband is the sole breadwinner and I am the homemaker. He gives me money for the week. It sounds old fashioned, but it works for us. I don't feel any less of a woman. My confidence and self-esteem are not associated with or influenced by my income. I work hard in the household and I do a good job. We have adjusted and can comfortably survive with this routine, as we have for over six years.'

— Claudia (36), mum to Aaron (six) and Cadee (three)

'If you have to ask for money from your husband to buy a coffee and some pads, you might as well put up the red flag. If this is not what you are used to, you have to sort out the finances before you retreat to the dark ages when women had no financial control or independence.'

— Jane (32), mum to Chance (two)

Women today have thriving careers and many earn more than their male counterparts. This makes the new financial situation even harder to deal with. For myself, by no longer being financially independent I felt another part of my personality slipping away. I needed to change things so that I could still enjoy life as I knew it, release the guilt of spending and reclaim some financial liberty. Seriously, how many times can you feed your family baked beans for dinner so you can afford a new pair of shoes? (That's a joke. I never did this, though my husband would argue otherwise.)

To improve the situation, my husband and I sat down and worked out exactly how much was coming in and what was going out. We established a budget that could accommodate some treats we were used to, like going out for a weekly meal and the occasional weekend away. Then we decided against expenses that were unreasonable for now, such as luxury holidays, kitchen and garden renovations and car upgrades. Lastly, we agreed to a budget I was responsible for to fund household expenses and some ... female essentials (pampering treatments, clothes, shoes ...). We organised a weekly direct deposit to my bank account to cover these expenses.

I also started making more of an effort to contribute to long-term bigger financial decisions. Admittedly, this was something I had never had an active interest in before. I learned more about our situation and dissected different financial scenarios that influenced our future. It provided me with a greater sense of control and understanding of our financial expectations.

That discussion was a relief in itself. My husband and I were on the same page. Having some personal financial freedom made me more independent and, as a result, happier, because I felt a little more like myself again and confident the bills would still get paid. I also had a better sense of how we could best raise our family and be financially in control of our future for the long term, not just while I was on maternity leave.

In hindsight, you would think we would have discussed all these details before we had a child. But we were so focused on having the child that we neglected to *really* think about other serious factors. And to be fair, you don't always know what is going to bother you until after the event. Better late than never!

By being open with one another, we spoke honestly about how we were living and coping financially at this phase of our lives and could start thinking realistically about how we wanted to live and cope financially going forward.

'For a few months, I had allowed myself to be a kept woman with the man of the household responsible for and totally in control of the finances. After trying this role out for a few months, I discovered it made me feel uncomfortable. There are many women who are happy to abandon any control and still feel happy, confident and self-assured in their roles. But I am not one of these women.'

— Marian (34), mum to Candace (four) and Brett (one)

Even the closest of girlfriends are reluctant to discuss money, spending habits and how to adjust to a reduced income. You don't often have an open discussion with others about how they are coping with the change. Money is a taboo subject and something we are too proud to discuss with others out of fear of looking inadequate and anything other than secure and financially comfortable. It's also a difficult topic to bring up when you know the mums around you clearly have more money than you and don't care about budgeting.

'We have this mum in our circle of friends who is rich and doesn't have to sacrifice or budget. She wanted to organise a weekend away with all the families and nominated an expensive hotel to stay at. It was too expensive for us, but I was too embarrassed to say no. But another mum just turned to her and said, "Sorry, but we can't afford it right now."

It was so refreshing to hear her honesty and made me more comfortable to say it as well when conversations arose about buying or doing something. The reality is that some of us have to watch what we spend. That's life.'

— Samantha (32), mum to Adrian (four), Gordana (two) and Tahlia (six months)

There can be a lot of competition between mums as most want to appear as if they have everything together. You may feel like you are the only one who has to think twice about an expense, but you are not alone. You are not the only woman who has to walk straight past a $300 coat you would have purchased impulsively only months earlier, do your own hair colour and look out for work-from-home opportunities to bring in some extra funds. There are millions of mums who only shop at sale time, frequent discount shops and forego a meal out for coffee and cake instead.

'We sacrificed eating out, landscape gardening and a new TV. Once I found something else to replace the feeling these things gave me, it didn't hurt so much.'

— Marika (34), mum to Fotini and Spiridon (three)

'I don't know why people complain. I have learnt the smartest budgeting tips that give us the flexibility to still holiday, eat out and treat ourselves so that we don't really feel deprived.'

— Tanya (34), mum to Charlie (three)

Living with one less income is something you can adjust to. There are some tips to make the process easier, such as learning to be more resourceful, adopting smarter spending habits and staying actively involved in the finances to retain a sense of control. So, with a few adjustments, you can still live and enjoy your life as you knew it and be lucky enough to be home with the baby.

How to adjust to a reduced income

- Educate yourself on the financial health of your family so you know if and for how long you can stay at home to care for your children.
- Discuss with your partner how much money is coming in versus going out.
- Set and agree to some spending boundaries.

- Still treat yourselves but with smaller things, less often.
- Gratefully accept the benefits your situation has to offer, until you are ready to make changes like downgrading your house or returning to work.

Thirty painless money-saving tips to help you survive maternity leave

1. Research the eligibility of any government assistance that is available to families.
2. Sell items you no longer need for treats you do.
3. Buy in bulk.
4. Shop at sale time.
5. Create and stick to a budget or speak with a professional to guide you.
6. Refinance any loan repayments to reduce expenses where possible while you are on maternity leave.
7. Give up a non-essential daily or weekly habit.
8. Stretch hair appointments.
9. Start a business from home or look at work-from-home employment options.
10. Look out for promotions in your letterbox or local paper for services that offer discounts or free extras on certain days of the week.
11. Learn to make your own face masks and lotions instead of going to a professional.
12. Get a new wardrobe and enjoy a social night out for free by hosting a clothes swapping party with friends and neighbours.
13. Instead of going to the professionals for your hair colour, tanning, waxing, pampering treatments, try some of the do-it-yourself products on the market.
14. Instead of going out for dinner, go out for coffee, split a meal or stick

with just a snack so you still get the restaurant experience, without the expense.

15. Entertain the family by scouring the internet or newspaper for free or very cheap seminars to attend, markets to visit, courses to complete and concerts to hear.

16. Ask for discounts, even if they are not advertised.

17. Make your own cleaning products instead of spending a fortune on branded ones.

18. Register for free on websites that regularly communicate savings tips.

19. Buy second hand where possible.

20. Cook in bulk and freeze meals to avoid another expensive trip to the supermarket.

21. Shop with a list to avoid impulse purchases.

22. Don't use credit cards.

23. Review health, car and house insurance policies as well as any telecommunications and utilities services and shop around for better deals.

24. Swap services and products with other families.

25. If you always purchase the same magazines, subscribe instead as it is much cheaper.

26. Borrow instead of buy what you can, such as books, magazines and DVDs.

27. Cancel unused memberships such as gym membership. It is cheaper to pay casual rates when you do go than it is to pay a set weekly fee when you don't.

28. Buy generic brands for groceries and medications.

29. Enter competitions, redeem free samples or register with reputable market research groups that pay you for your time or provide free product to answer some questions.

30. Research the best prices before you make any large ticket purchases.

CHAPTER 16

... is for 'Nurturing yourself'

'You are not a bad mother if you sometimes put your own needs first.'

— Mikki (34), mum to Markus (two)

This chapter discusses what you need to do for yourself to better cope with motherhood, and why it's imperative you take responsibility for *you*. It also includes ways to nurture yourself to be the best mum you can be. From the moment you fall pregnant and forever thereafter you will feel so much pressure, expectation and judgement to parent a certain way. How you deliver the baby, feed him, settle him, whether you put him in child care, what age you send him to school and even what nappies you use will all be scrutinised. It is difficult, draining and stressful keeping up with everything you are supposed to do, especially if you always try to follow the parenting books' advice and what other well-meaning mothers recommend.

As you devote practically every moment to caring for a new life, there are many times when you will feel as if your own sanity and general wellbeing are on the line as a result. This is unless you are a) not human, b) have much more help than you need or c) are just too damn good. Regardless, most new mums don't sleep, wash, rest or eat anywhere near as much as they should to be at their best for the long run.

Being a mother is a full-time job that leaves you with little time or energy to nurture the woman behind the mum. Physically, you are running around after your children, making sure they are safe, entertained and organised. Mentally, all you do is think about them, what they need, how you can assist their development, and ways you can be a better mother. Emotionally, you battle feelings of inadequacy and doubt, unless you have unwavering self-confidence and the (unrealistic) ability to never slip up.

Becoming a parent is the biggest life change you could ever experience. This is the time of your life when *you* need to be nurtured most as your emotions, mind and body are at their most vulnerable. Yet, ironically, it is also the time when you are most neglected. You don't have anything left to give to yourself and everybody around you is also focused on loving, nurturing and attending to the baby instead.

You probably feel that's the way things should be too! You might feel guilty and selfish even contemplating doing something for yourself. However, parenting is the hardest job in the world, so you need to ensure you are fit mentally, physically and emotionally. Too much personal neglect and you risk falling apart, either inside or out. You can very quickly turn into an angry, unwashed, stressed, frumpy, resentful and perpetually tired woman, sporting dark circles under her eyes, a soiled top and looking like she has the weight of the world on her shoulders. And when that happens, you can no longer be the best parent you can be to your child or the best person you can be for yourself.

So to continue to be your best while you deal with the ongoing dramas that motherhood throws at you, you must listen and respond to what your mind and body need. Only then can you really take care of yourself as a person and be better equipped to take care of your child. Tune in to your happiness and wellbeing. Make sure you feel balanced, and if not, make it a priority to restore order within you.

Motherhood is for life and your work will never be completely finished, so learn to accommodate your needs along with those of your family. You can still nourish your mind, body and attitude while being a wonderful mum, not at the expense of it. Of course, if you have just come home from the hospital, taking up tai chi might be a challenge and you will need time to recover before embarking on anything too adventurous. As you adjust to being a mother, just take small steps to nurture yourself until you are back to your best.

Obviously, post-baby, nurturing yourself requires extra effort and energy, but the results are worth it. Pre-baby, you had more time and motivation to care for you without having to prioritise a baby. You could rest, relax and pamper a tired, stressed body. You could start a course and instigate new career moves to stimulate a restless mind in as little as a weekend. And you could holiday and leisure anywhere to rejuvenate when you were feeling depleted. Life was more about you.

When you fell pregnant, you still had the time and motivation for yourself, plus a team of people willing to nurture you as well. Partners, parents, siblings, colleagues and friends all went the extra mile to ensure you were taken care of. Everybody wants to do something for the pregnant woman. You could sit back and enjoy the extra love and attention. Unfortunately, it's easy to fall into a false sense of security that people will always be bending over backwards to care for you.

'When I fell pregnant for the first time, my family went out of their way to ensure I was always comfortable, healthy and happy. They saw to it that I had everything I wanted and needed for a smooth, successful pregnancy.

They were quick to provide extra pillows to support my back, the "comfortable" chair to sit on and the extra serving of dessert. They also strongly insisted I never helped with the washing up.

I was carrying their first grandchild after all and they didn't want me straining in any way. This pregnancy was all about me. I felt so nurtured. So loved. So taken care of.

However, I can't believe how quickly everything turned once I gave birth! I was clearly no longer the centre of attention. People didn't really care where I was sitting, what I was eating, how I was feeling, what I did that day and how they could better "nurture" me. All of a sudden, all anybody ever wanted to know was how was the baby feeling? What did the baby want? What did the baby do today? I no longer mattered. Everybody's effort, time, concern and attention was now going towards the baby.'

— Emily (29), mum to Angus (one)

When you have the baby you find that all the people who once ran to help you barely remember your name. Everybody is focused on the baby. While people are offering to help, it is to better nurture the baby, not you. You no longer matter the way you did. Therefore, unless you have an insistent partner or family member forcing you to rest and rejuvenate, taking care of yourself is once again your responsibility.

'I don't mind and perhaps expected that all the fuss would be on the baby. I would have just liked a little warning that change would be sudden.

I wish I knew to enjoy all the extra fuss during pregnancy because in a blink of an eye all that love, support and nurturing is transferred to the baby. People will call to ask about the baby. People will visit to see the baby. People will do anything for the baby. And sometimes they won't even ask about or barely acknowledge you. If you want something for yourself, you have to speak up or get it on your own.'

— Tara (33), mum to Angus (four) and Jenna (one)

Taking care of yourself is the responsible thing to do for yourself, your family and, importantly, your child. If you feel nurtured you will have more patience, strength, positivity and energy to cope better in your role as a mum. Of course, you can still fulfil the role of mum without properly taking care of yourself, but at what expense? Can you honestly be as patient, strong, positive and energetic a parent as you want to be? Nourishing and nurturing yourself can be as simple as having daily hot baths or a regular babysitter, enrolling in a university course or embarking on a new career. Only you know what you really need to do to feel better as a person.

'People say, once you have kids, you won't remember life beforehand. I must be alone as I reminisce about waking up late on the weekends whenever I felt like it, taking hours to read through the Sunday papers and lounging on the couch reading a book for as long as I liked.

Then there were the afternoons I would waste shopping and bonding with girlfriends, the mornings I spent having a pampering pedicure or manicure and the massages I found time for.

My heart fills with love at the sound of my baby squealing or the sight of him smiling, but there are times when I just want to be left alone to enjoy some quiet time for myself.'

— Miranda (35), mum to Drew (six) and Henry (one)

Fifty practical, effective ways to nurture yourself while raising a family

1. Go for a walk to clear the mind.
2. Buy yourself a treat for no reason.
3. Find some alone time every day, even 30 minutes.
4. Develop a close circle of friends and family you can talk to and rely on.
5. Be more intimate with your partner, even if it's for more hugs, kisses and talks.
6. Indulge in what you enjoy, such as reading magazines or eating chocolate.
7. Have regular relaxing baths.
8. Plan an affordable getaway or holiday.
9. Indulge in beauty treatments.
10. Develop interests outside family commitments.
11. Spend time alone with your partner.
12. Make an effort to see friends and family.
13. Experiment with spirituality, meditation and relaxation classes.
14. Take regular naps.
15. Buy yourself flowers.
16. Learn to say no.
17. Remind yourself what makes you happy.
18. Join a support group.
19. Find a mentor.
20. Exercise regularly.
21. Give yourself rewards when you achieve things.
22. Ask for help or outsource when life is too demanding.

23. Become more optimistic and change any negative thoughts to positive.
24. Reflect often on your achievements, hopes and dreams.
25. Make changes to parts of your life that need improvement.
26. Give yourself praise and encouragement.
27. Don't sweat the small stuff.
28. Write down dreams, goals and wishes.
29. Put goals into action.
30. Accomplish something you would be proud of.
31. Try new things and experiences.
32. Learn a new skill.
33. Do more of what makes you feel good about yourself.
34. Review career options.
35. Spend more time with people who empower and inspire you.
36. Treasure, reflect on and really 'take in' the quality moments with your child.
37. Renew old interests or hobbies you truly enjoyed a lifetime ago.
38. Test and stretch your limits.
39. Buy new underwear.
40. Create an inspiration board.
41. Get a babysitter more often.
42. Let go of guilty feelings.
43. Do one nice thing for yourself every day.
44. Pamper yourself regularly, even if it's just by putting on perfume, body lotion or make-up.
45. Laugh more by spending time with certain people or watching funny movies.
46. Eat your favourite comfort food.
47. Start a course.
48. Call a friend.

49. Eat well to keep your body and your mind fit and healthy.

50. Remember all the things you appreciate and love and all the potential you have.

Nurturing ourselves can be incredibly rewarding. It will make us feel happier, healthier, more balanced, confident and satisfied that we are fit parents and complete individuals. It doesn't have to be expensive or time consuming. It just needs to be a priority and a part of your life for it to make a difference to your health, attitude and general wellbeing, and how well you respond to all the highs and lows that motherhood will throw at you.

The four-step process to nurturing you

Step 1: Find some quiet time to reflect on different areas of your life, such as your health, mental stimulation, emotions.

Step 2: Write down what part of your life feels neglected. For example, your body might be rundown, your mind bored with the baby routine or emotions affected by bouts of anxiety.

Step 3: Make some changes to address your needs. You might start alternating night feeds with your partner, enrol in a course or join a support group.

Step 4: Regularly review your needs and re-visit step 1.

CHAPTER 17

... is for 'Organisational skills'

So, your husband has returned to work, your mum to her home and the visitors are starting to subside. You can now fully concentrate on bonding with baby and finding normality. But what is normal? Is it normal to have laundry spilling out to the back verandah, an empty fridge, no recollection of your last shower, and not a free moment to pay a bill or return a call? A few weeks of this and you won't even be able to find your way to the front door. And this is just the beginning.

What are you going to do in a few months' time when you might have plans to return to work, intend to complete some further studies or have high hopes of throwing your husband a huge fortieth birthday party? How do you start planning next month when you don't even know what day it is? You feel like you are always chasing your tail and don't know what you are supposed to do first. You know you are continuously busy with no time for you, yet by the end of the day you have no idea what you've actually done.

> 'I can't believe I used to spend one hour getting ready to go out. I have now perfected the two-minute shower, the ten-minute make-up and the 60-second up-do. I can eat while I'm cooking, sleep when I'm on the toilet and shovel a ton of toys into the spare room before the doorbell even stops ringing. Who would have thought I'd be this organised?'
>
> — Lorna (34), mum to Kyle (six) and Amie (three)

Welcome to your new life. One filled with mayhem, madness and far too many demands for a single day. Some days will be smoother than others and you will be able to rest, catch up around the house, go for a walk and cook dinner. On other days you will find yourself still in your nightwear at 4 p.m. Either way, making the most of the time in the day to feel like you've actually accomplished something will be one of your greatest challenges.

> 'My husband would come home and the place would be a mess. I would have only just got out of my sleepwear. Dinner was takeaway and his underwear drawers were always empty. It was hard to explain that it was just one of those days. I know that I wasn't sleeping all day or watching the TV soaps. I didn't even know what I did all day, but somehow the day slipped by and I had nothing to show for it.'
>
> — Tonya (36), mum to Kaylan (three) and Dylan (one)

You are not the only one. Lack of time to get through all the daily challenges is a key stress trigger and something most mothers experience all too often. It can leave us feeling overwhelmed. When there is too much to do, it is easy to have a panic reaction and half-heartedly try to do a little bit of everything, without really achieving anything.

You are left feeling defeated that nothing got done. Soon you start believing everything is too hard and you don't even bother. A vicious cycle begins and the laundry continues to pile up.

As a new parent, family responsibilities will become one of your main priorities, at least in the beginning. With sharpened organisational skills, you can adjust to this change in priorities and actually feel reasonably satisfied with what you are achieving. First you need to learn how to organise yourself to get through the early weeks of parenthood. Then you need to learn how to competently manage the ongoing demands in your new life for the future.

Even if you were previously one of those women who wasn't big on making or sticking to plans and preferred to take things as they come, you will find that being organised will actually streamline the day or week and make you more efficient. By being organised you will feel more in control and optimistic about your day. You will develop a bit of a system, or routine, for everything that needs to get done. This will give you a way to manage the house, the baby, your needs and other things well, with greater ease.

Ten benefits to getting organised

1. Get more done.
2. Have more balance.
3. Be more productive.
4. Be more successful at setting and achieving goals.
5. Have a clearer sense of priorities and purpose.
6. Have more time for yourself.
7. Have more time for those you love.
8. Enjoy a calmer environment.
9. End up with a healthier state of mind.
10. Feel more satisfied and happy with what you are achieving.

How to organise yourself in the first few months

'I know it sounds impossible, but I did not leave the house for nearly five weeks. And I mean I did not go for a walk, out for coffee or for a drive. I just couldn't. It took me a long time to confidently organise myself and the baby so that I could go out, get things done and start living my new life. Once I got some help organising myself, the house and my baby, I did not feel so overwhelmed and I actually got more done. Now that I am due for my second one, I know it is not going to take me a month to find the front door.'

— Veronica (29), mum to Penny (two)

Priorities and the way you organise them into your day will change as your newborn grows and you heal mentally, physically and emotionally. In the short term, life is about surviving the little things and taking care of yourself and the baby so that you are both fit and healthy for the future.

Ten steps to feeling more organised in the early weeks of motherhood

1. Prioritise feeling healthy and rested so you have the stamina to organise the day.
2. Deal with one baby phase at a time and organise your routine on a week-by-week basis as there are many changes happening in the beginning.
3. Ask for help and delegate where possible before you have a meltdown.
4. Speak to other mums about their routine and what works for them.

5. Try different routines until you figure out what works best for you and the baby.
6. Prioritise what you must do for the day or the week and let go of everything else.
7. Plan your day in blocks; i.e. morning: shower; midday: prepare dinner; afternoon: walk.
8. Stay focused by writing a list of five key things you want to achieve for the day, and keep this list visible to remind you when you are tempted to do something else with your valuable time.
9. Be flexible and accept that even the most organised plans can and will fold.
10. Some days you won't be able to deal with organising anything and that is okay.

In the beginning, organise yourself to have more rest and extra help in your day. Rest and help will enable you to slowly adjust to your new life and avoid too many meltdowns. After you have recovered and found your rhythm, the way you organise your life will change. Only then can you start to be more ambitious.

How to organise yourself for the future

You will once again be able to fit in more of the things you were used to doing, such as socialising, networking, exercising, indulging in a hobby and perhaps even working or studying. Time restraints will always be part of your life now, but by getting better at the juggling act, you can still take advantage of the opportunities around you and look at what else you want to do away from caring for the home and children. The trick is to be more selective about how you invest your time, as you don't have any to waste! It will be very tempting to try to be a supermum and do everything you think you should, but 'having it all' has some drawbacks. While women do have more skills, opportunities and expectations than ever before, it is a constant battle to achieve what we want and still feel happy and balanced in the process.

'It took about six months, but I actually started to feel a little bored with the baby and homemaker routine. I was itching to do something else to stimulate me. I went from baby routine to starting a business, looking for part-time work, investigating courses I could do and getting my body back in shape. After a few months I realised I was pushing things too far and feeling stressed. I had to cut back. I thought I could do it all, but I couldn't.'

— Liz (38), mum to Baily (five) and Morris (three)

Instead of trying to do and have everything you think a perfect family should do and have, think about what would make you most satisfied with *your* self and *your* life. Review your core values and organise yourself based on your values, rather than trying to keep up with what other people are doing or what you think is expected in society today.

It's a lot of pressure to care for the children, work, maintain the house, enjoy a full social life, regular exercise routine and pursue a night-time business venture. And don't forget there are also extracurricular activities for you and the children, regular holidays, a full night's sleep, and quality time spent with family and friends. This sort of pace in life is not sustainable for the long term without some consequences.

Even without doing all of the above there is still plenty to do. It makes sense to focus precious time and energy on the most important aspects of your life that will bring you happiness and satisfaction. Then simply let go of what you can live without. There is no point in aspiring to everything if the process is too stressful and the journey unrewarding.

'I know I am an educated, smart, capable woman and I can achieve many great things. But I have to accept I just can't do everything that I want, right now. I am still working towards my dreams, but realistically it's going to take me longer to achieve these things now that I am juggling family life as well. (Most days) I'm okay with that.

For now I just want to be with my kids. When they reach school age, I will do more for myself. If I try to take on too much I doubt I would do a good job with too much on. And I wouldn't even enjoy myself. For me, it's not worth the extra headache, not right now.

I believe I can have it all, just not simultaneously. For now I am only focusing on a few priorities at a time.'

— Toni (34), mum to Angus (three) and Annette (one)

Be realistic about your resources, expectations and what you really can get done in your day, week, month and overall life journey. Be pragmatic and accept that being a parent does come with sacrifices and restrictions. Without time, money and resources, we just can't do everything we want to do when we want it. Accept this, adjust to the changes and organise your life differently until you find what works for you.

'Family life is now my priority. But it is not all I want or value. I value friendships, a life outside the home and more financial security. Therefore, I organise my life to have these things because they are a great source of happiness for me.'

— Tia (33), mum to Destiny (two)

'Past generations had more help and sometimes fewer demands. Today we are doing more and expecting more for ourselves. Unfortunately, we don't have the same support as our parents had in terms of grandparents and other family members available to help. It's hard and impossible to do it all.'

— Courtney (28), mum to Sarah (one)

Once you accept you can't do it all on your own, figure out what you can do best or how you can do what matters. Instead of striving for perfection and aspiring to do everything, strive to have some sort of balance and work on doing fewer things better. There will always be a contest between different priorities, so stay focused on organising yourself around what is most important to you.

Top tips for organising your life

- Figure out what you value most in life, such as family time, money, friendships.
- Write down what you want to get done for the day based on your priorities.
- Prepare in advance.
- Be flexible when things don't work out exactly as planned.

To do

_____

_____

_____

_____

_____

CHAPTER 18

... is for 'Positive thinking'

'A positive attitude brings happiness, strength, energy and motivation —
everything a woman needs to survive motherhood.'

— Arabella (36), mum to Cairo (three)

People continue to write about, talk about and study the power of positive thinking because it is the backbone to controlling your outlook and ultimately your destiny. As a new mum, your life has exploded to include many more responsibilities. You will need all the optimism you can muster to see you through the daily challenges and personal doubts and to get closer to realising your dreams for the future. It makes sense to understand the fundamentals behind positive thinking, the benefits it can lead to, and how an overworked mum can use it to achieve great things for her life and attitude.

As a mum living a completely alien life to that of only a few months earlier, there are many frustrating moments to contend with. You may even feel resentful or unsatisfied with your routine, lifestyle and dreams, and wonder why things didn't turn out as expected. This is normal and you are not the first mum to admit that life is not all about *Oprah* specials and morning social coffees.

Life can easily become all about never-ending chores, constant nagging, a mundane routine, lack of funds, a grizzly baby and a quickly disappearing waist, love life, social life and ambition. Things can spiral out of control from the moment you come home from the hospital to discover three-day-old dishes and an unmade bed, pre-baby clothes that do not miraculously fit and an email from a colleague announcing she just got your dream job. You feel a little ripped off. Even if you have an angelic cherub with your dimples and long eyelashes gurgling at you, there may be a niggling feeling within that makes you dream of more order, freedom and fulfilment in your life.

While there will be good times, just as there will be bad times, it's easy to find yourself feeling negative and deflated sometimes as you adjust to the new you and new life. You are alone, inexperienced and facing unknown terrain. But you don't have to let these feelings affect your attitude or expectations for the future.

'Do not let circumstances influence your thoughts and moods. By rising over them mentally, you will eventually rise over them materially.'

— Remez Sasson

Millions of mothers across the world manage to raise happy children, maintain organised households, nurture personal interests and friendships, and fulfil hopes, dreams and values that matter to them. They too probably found themselves drowning in nappy soaker and going though a pre-midlife crisis of their own, but they got through it all and learned, laughed and lived to tell their stories.

The first step to being more like these successful, satisfied and capable women and mothers is to embrace a more positive opinion. Like them, learn to believe in yourself, what you are capable of, and let go of the negativity that is holding you back from a bright future. Surround yourself with others who share your outlook and fine-tune your mindset to replace negative thoughts with positive. A glass-half-full attitude will strengthen your confidence and self-esteem so you can stretch yourself to achieve great things.

The benefits of being positive

- Growing confidence.
- Can-do attitude.
- Positive self-esteem.
- General happiness.
- Healthy mind and body.
- Feeling of fulfilment and knowing everything really is okay.
- Achieve your goals.
- Overcome stressful feelings and situations faster and more efficiently.
- Increased energy because you are not drained by negativity.
- Deeper relationships as people naturally want to spend more time with you.
- A more organised home, life and thought process.
- Luck seems to come your way more often.
- No fears holding you back from enjoying life and the opportunities surrounding you.

Ten ways to be a positive thinker

The first step to being a positive mother is to *genuinely* believe that you are a happy mum and woman. Identify a personal mantra such as: 'I am positive, I think positive and I act positive.'

'Affirm the positive, visualise the positive and expect the positive and your life will change accordingly.'

— Remez Sasson

Be objective and neutral about the bad stuff. Don't dwell on the disappointments of your past so they don't diminish the hope you have for the future. Just because you couldn't breastfeed the first time, that doesn't mean you shouldn't even try the second time. Or just because you didn't get the first job you applied for that doesn't mean you shouldn't even bother applying for any others.

Build a support network of other positive mums, friends and confidantes in your life who share an uplifting energy. Stay away from or limit your time with people who drag you down. A supportive mothers' group, partner or relative will inspire and motivate you and carry you through moments of doubt.

'I suffer depression, so when I feel down, I'm really down. Only mums who have experienced depression, or know someone who has, can understand how over-powering depression is. You are consumed with negative feelings and they strongly weigh down on your mind and body. I'll crash, burn, overeat, cry and generally give up. I really struggle to pick myself up and feel positive again on my own.

However, I don't want to be down. I want to be a positive, motivated and driven person. To pick myself up when I'm down and reignite some optimism, I rely on a support group whom I meet with on a fortnightly basis, plus a close group of friends who understand me and know what kind, sympathetic and encouraging words I need to hear to get back up in the saddle.

The people I surround myself with help to steer me around the hurdles and put my mindset back into perspective. Then I can keep moving forward.'

— Sandy (40), mum to Tony (eleven) and Mick (seven)

Have a healthy body. If you take care of your body, it will take care of your mind. Rest when you are overtired, walk when you are emotional and eat well to fuel your positive thinking. It will be much easier to handle feeding problems, reflux and ambitious home business plans when your body is strong and your mind prepared.

Be more conscious of what you are telling yourself, because that is what you will end up believing. It takes the same energy to be positive as it does to be negative, yet it is the positive attitude that breeds positive results. When you find yourself battling thoughts such as, 'This is too hard', or 'I'm never going to get my body back', or 'I'm too dumb for anyone to employ me', change your words and focus. Think, 'It's not the hardest thing I've done or will do', 'I will lose it 1 kilo at a time', and 'With my skills and experiences, any employee is lucky to have me.'

'I'm a positive person most of the time, but I'm still human and have some bad days. I don't always win contracts I apply for, my toddler does hate me some days, I get offended by my mother-in-law's criticism and occasionally I have to unbutton my pants when I sit.

Of course these things upset me, but I have learnt to take them in my stride, grieve a little then move towards making a positive difference.

I'll celebrate when I do get a contract, distract my daughter when she is having a tantrum, stay away from the mother-in-law when she gets on my nerves and go for an extra walk when I feel fat. I have learnt you can do something positive to overcome a negative feeling or experience.'

— Elly (35), mum to Linda (four) and Susie (one)

Don't give up after a setback. You will have days when you are worn out, emotional and feeling down, just as you will have days where you are bouncing off the walls with energy, in control and happy in the moment. Be patient with yourself. A positive mindset is a lifelong habit that brings lifelong benefits. Don't expect your whole life to revolutionise after one day of thinking positively. And don't think one bad day will dictate the future.

Be conscious of the vibes you are sending out. You might not realise that you are coming across as insecure, aggressive or doubtful. You need to think positive to be able to act positive and achieve positive things.

'Have you heard the quote "what we fear, we create"? After hearing this and really paying attention, I realised that is exactly what I was doing and how I was living my life.

After six years at home with the kids I found myself battling anxiety, low self-esteem and isolation. My confidence was at an all-time low and all I could think about was that I was going nowhere fast — except to a very expensive naturopath to buy some very expensive anti-anxiety herbs and vitamins.

I started taking small steps to change things in my life, starting with my diet and exercise. This immediately made me feel healthier and happier. Then I found the confidence to spend more time in society and formed closer relationships with other positive people. These people were so confident, vibrant and striving for great things in their life for themselves and their family. They weren't limiting themselves with their insecurities or any doubts.

They inspired me to believe I have what it takes to start a business. This was always a small wish I kept hidden to myself because I never thought I was smart enough to do it and I didn't want people to laugh at me.

For a time there I really was going nowhere, because this is what I believed. Yet, one thought and one action led to another and I did, and do, feel transformed. I am more positive now about myself and my future and good things are starting to happen.'

— Josephine (37), mum to Billy (six) and Ebony (two)

Look at life, its challenges, dramas and hiccups in a positive light. We are all faced with unfortunate outcomes, people and situations at times. Rather than be afraid and resentful, focus on the good that can come of it. If your employer won't have you back on a part-time basis, don't be disheartened. Instead, think how this is a great time to investigate a different career path. If the first-choice childcare centre can't accommodate your child for another eighteen years, don't think you will never find anything that suits. Instead, look into alternative care and how it might be even better suited. There's always a positive take to every negative if you look for it.

Start being more positive today and make it part of your attitude going forward. Being positive won't automatically bring the golden opportunity to your doorstep, but it will open your eyes to a world that is full of them.

Remember: if nothing changes, nothing changes. If your old attitude hasn't brought you the success you want, try a different approach and adopt a more positive, can-do, and will-achieve attitude. Then see what happens.

CHAPTER 19

Q
... is for 'Questions'

Even though we are all different, there are many common questions most of us find ourselves asking at one point or another. Here are some of them. Hopefully the answers will alleviate any doubts in your mind and reassure you that what you are thinking and how you are acting are completely normal and expected at this point in your life.

1. Will I get bored with the stay-at-home mum routine and how do I deal with it?
2. How do I cope with the baby blues?
3. How long will it take to lose the baby weight and reclaim my body?
4. Will motherhood change me as a person?
5. Is it normal to feel lonely?

6. How do I handle the guilt that comes with motherhood?

7. How should I involve my partner more?

Will I get bored with the stay-at-home mum routine and how do I deal with it?

The stay-at-home mum routine will be different from your working environment for obvious reasons. You are not dealing with as many adults and your mind is being stimulated differently. You are no longer in an environment where there is someone to motivate, empower, congratulate or encourage you. This can make some days a little routine and, dare we say it … boring.

It doesn't mean, however, that the only way you can combat boredom is to get a job. It means you need to stimulate your mind more to make the day and journey more rewarding and interesting. You can do this by exploring services your community offers, such as free seminars and entertainment. You can spend more time with other mothers who can provide emotional support and inspiration. You can look at how you can use your work skills for things such as volunteering. Or you might want to just enjoy the boredom while you can, because it certainly doesn't last long.

'After nearly ten months I started to get really bored and spoke to my employer about returning to work before my maternity leave ended, but they could not accommodate me earlier than my original date. I am so relieved it didn't work out because two weeks later my baby's routine completely changed and she started doing new things. It made me realise I'm not ready to go to work yet. I still wanted and needed to be a proactive parent in her life. I recommend you don't rush into doing anything too drastic at the first sign of boredom.'

— Anoula (31), mum to Henrietta (one)

Boredom isn't always such a bad thing. It will give you the opportunity to rest. It is not often you will find time to do something for yourself, and these small windows provide the perfect opportunity to explore things you always meant to but never had time for. If you don't feel like resting, use the time to do something completely different to what you have been doing all day. This will help you change focus to re-invigorate your mind and relieve you from the stress of cooking, cleaning and babysitting all day.

'Every night while my partner bathed the baby, I would head into the shed, put some music on and paint. It used to clear my mind and it felt nice to indulge in a pleasurable pastime.'

— Monica (39), mum to Hannah (four) and Thomas (one)

If you find your routine has started to open up more pockets of time for yourself, seize the chance to get involved in a new interest or pursue a subject you are naturally drawn to. Or you could help a charity, a local business or get involved in an industry you always dreamed of. It doesn't always need to take you away from your responsibilities at home. You can work on plans or reports from home, make phone calls or just limit the hours you can realistically spare. Either way, you will reclaim the sense of fulfilment that using your mind differently offers and break up your week at the same time.

'I was home with the baby and thinking about how hard it is on some women and how some mums struggle with the routine and staying motivated. Without a second thought, I called the local council, met up with the course director and launched a series of motivational seminars for mums that I would host. It felt great to have something else to focus on and be able to put my skills to good use.'

— Courtenay (35), mum to Gia (four) and Callum (two)

What other mums do to stimulate their minds

- Join playgroups.
- Join mothers' groups.
- Go to community events.
- Study.
- Work.
- Volunteer at kinder or school.
- Shop.
- Exercise.
- Use the internet more.
- Meditate.
- Change their routine.
- Keep in contact with friends.
- Schedule more 'me time'.
- Get of the house more often.

How do I cope with the baby blues?

You will have days where you feel tearful, rundown and snowed under by everything you are responsible for. Not only are you taking care of your baby or perhaps other children as well, but you are cooking, cleaning and trying your best to be on top of all your family's needs. You never seem to stop, and before you know it, the day is over and you have to start all over again tomorrow. There is just no end in sight. When your husband comes home, he's too exhausted to relieve you and all you want to do is throw in the towel and run away for a few days.

This is enough to make anyone feel uninspired at times. It's an entirely normal reaction. How can anyone do this day in, day out without feeling blue every now and again and frustrated with everything on their plate? You might not be depressed, but you probably feel neglected, unappreciated and a little down.

'I'm always tired. The baby is wearing me out big time. All I seem to do is clean, wash, iron, cook, nurse, burp, settle, blah blah blah. Then, I do the same thing the next day. My partner comes home late, which I hate because I have to deal with the 5–7 p.m. feral hours on my own. I don't care how hard he works — I still need him to help me. Am I the only one with this problem??? I feel like I am supposed to be superwoman but I just can't do it. I am going crazy here and sometime I have to have a good cry to get it all out of my system. As much as I love my husband and the baby, there are days I just want to run away by myself.'

— Stavroula (32), mum to Emmanuelle (one)

Many women will experience these feelings. After childbirth, some level of stress and fatigue is normal and can make you feel worse about life and your situation. To deal with the baby blues and get over them, some women need to seek professional help. Others implement tactics, such as the ones listed below, to lift their spirits and give them the strength to overcome these emotions and feel more positive again. Here are some suggestions to help:

- Talk to your partner.
- See your doctor.
- Get some help around the house.
- Get some help with the baby.
- Free up more time for yourself every day to relax.
- Participate in a support network, either online or face to face.
- Listen to some relaxation music.
- Remind yourself this is normal and will pass.

- Give yourself something to look forward to each day, week or month.
- Use affirmations and positive thinking to help you cope better with your moods.
- Get a good night's sleep and you'll find everything looks better in the morning.

How long will it take to lose the baby weight and reclaim my body?

'When I got pregnant I put on 18 kilos. Even though this was over the recommended weight gain, I felt glowing and gorgeous. Because I had such a positive self-esteem I didn't stress about it or wonder how on earth I was going to lose it again. I was confident that it would come off. It did.

Lots of exercise, a healthy diet and ten months later I was looking hot. I didn't mind that I didn't lose the weight straight away. The fact that the scales were slowly decreasing was motivation enough. I preferred not to stress about it and just enjoy being with my baby and reclaiming new clothes from my wardrobe each month.'

— Kristina (32), mum to Rafferty (two) and Colleen (one)

Every body and lifestyle is different and therefore each person loses weight at a different rate. Some women will put on 7 kilos and others 27 kilos — there is no magic formula. Similarly, there is no set timeframe for new mums to lose the baby weight. For some people the weight will just melt off without even trying. Others who are diligent with food and exercise may still struggle to lose the weight. The golden rule is that it takes nine months to put the weight on and it's absolutely fine and very common for it to take that long or longer to get it off again.

In a recent survey:

- 65 per cent of mums *expected* to lose their baby weight by the time their baby turned one, yet after the year, over half still had some weight to lose.
- 87 per cent of women say their stomach still hasn't returned to normal after losing the weight.
- 42 per cent of mothers gained more than the recommended amount of weight.
- Many new mothers assume that losing their baby fat will be much easier than it really is.

(Source: Babycenter.com, 'New Mom Body Survey: 7000 women tell it how it is'.)

It is most important that your body first recovers from being pregnant and the trauma of giving birth and that your mind adjusts to the enormity of your responsibilities. Only after dealing with these two things can you be fit enough mentally and physically to look at weight-loss strategies. The important thing is that you feel healthy and follow your doctor's instructions in terms of what you should be eating and how much exercise you should be doing at this point in your life.

Doctors and weight-loss practitioners can sit with you to discuss your lifestyle and weight-loss goals and devise a suggested plan and realistic timeframe in which to lose the weight — without compromising your health, breastfeeding requirements and lifestyle demands. However, most of the hard work will still be up to you. Losing weight and reclaiming your body takes determination, discipline, willpower and sheer effort. The time it takes to achieve your goal will depend a lot on when you feel ready to battle weight loss, and thereafter on where losing weight is on your priority list.

Give yourself permission to take your time as you adjust to the new factors in your life, and trust that the right eating plan and exercise program as part of your day-to-day lifestyle will enable you to get your body back eventually. There is no point in looking up to celebrity mums who are able to reclaim their pre-baby figures by the time they have left the hospital. They are supported by a team of chefs, fitness experts, babysitters and plastic surgeons who take most of the hard work out of the process.

'Stay organised, stay motivated, keep your trainers on and be real about what you can achieve.'

— Miranda (34), mum to Annabelle and Tracy (three)

Will motherhood change me as a person?

'Before I had children, I recall people (mainly my parents) saying to me, "One day when you have kids you will understand." It's like they were in this big secret club and the enormity and power it holds is too great to even begin to explain. Then I became a mum and got it, instantly. I felt like every childless person around me was walking around with rose-tinted glasses. Life and I would never, ever be the same again. It was now so much harder. It was more stressful and emotional yet one kiss from this healthy, innocent little miracle we created made it more fulfilling than anything else possibly could.'

— Lisbeth (41), mum to David (three)

Motherhood will change you to an extent. The new lifestyle factors will change you. Your new restrictions will change you. The gorgeous baby who greets you every morning with squeals of delight will change you. Even people who have children and are determined to live their lives exactly as they did before will have changed values, motivation and mindset.

You might keep the same personality, sense of humour, likes and dislikes, but you will also find yourself driven and fulfilled by different things now. Motherhood forces you to develop and grow as a person and this can be a very difficult, confronting process.

Sometimes it is easy for people to adjust to the new version of themselves, but others can struggle to accept that life and themselves will not and cannot be exactly the same as before. Your lifestyle is different; the demands and responsibilities you have are greater than ever before; your time is more precious; and you don't have the freedom you had to come and go, work and play, as you please. All these things shaped who you were. Now that they are different, you will be different.

'I struggled in the beginning because I never pre-empted that I would naturally change. I also didn't think that my new lifestyle and routine would change me. But it all did. I mourned a loss of identity work provided, resented the boredom and simplicity of the mummy routine and felt my brain cells disappear one nursery rhyme at a time, before I finally celebrated how motherhood could and did change me for the better.'

— Caroline (34), mum to Tallulah (three) and Aerin (one)

Once you accept that you are a different version of who you were pre-baby, it is easier to embrace the future and see how life can be more fulfilling than it was before. You just have to give yourself time to figure out what you now value and start making changes in your life and attitude that reflect what matters to you today.

Change can make people uncomfortable and nervous because it's often unknown, but change isn't always a bad thing. Sure, change, such as motherhood, does bring with it new adjustments and problems, but it also gives you new opportunities and an excuse to look at life differently and continue on a new journey, focusing on essentials and letting go of the superficial. It might be the same journey that you wanted pre-baby, but now it comes with a few roadblocks, pathways and hidden treasures you didn't see on the original map.

HOW MOTHERHOOD CHANGED REAL MUMS

For better	*For worse*
I aspire to be a great person and role model.	Less time for me so I am overweight and haggard.
My values in life are less superficial.	I yell more.
I have better time-management skills.	I can't be top in my career any longer.
I don't sweat the small stuff.	I worry all the time.
I enjoy simple pleasures more.	I am more emotional.
I feel more loved than ever before.	I have less money to indulge in things we used to.
I have rediscovered who I am.	Loss of identity.
I love my partner more.	Mundane daily routine.
I feel so blessed.	I have more responsibilities.

Is it normal to feel lonely?

In the build-up to giving birth, there seems to be an endless buzz around you. You are at work and everyone is commenting on how you are feeling and growing. Your friends all want to schedule a 'last' dinner/coffee/movie night to catch up before the baby arrives and your family continues to fuss around you. When you give birth you are worn out by the endless stream of visitors, demands from other children and the recovery process.

Finally, a few weeks later, the visitors subside, you feel a little better, your mum goes home, friends return to their own busy lives, and your partner goes back to work. You are stuck at home by yourself. No work. No friends. No family. No adult company. It's just you and a newborn who seems to sleep 80 per cent of the day. This is a massive emotional and physical adjustment.

This quiet time and the opportunity to be a homebody sounds good in theory, but realistically, instead of feeling happy, you can feel dramatically cut off from society and therefore lonely. One of the hardest things to get used to is a non-existent personal and social life, along with feeling sensitive, helpless and exhausted at the same time. It is especially difficult to cope if you are not close to a support network of family and friends.

'I can see why mums get lonely at home. The baby spends so much time sleeping and you tend to be at home a lot more than ever before. Then other days you feel so tired and helpless with an endlessly crying baby, and think everyone has things under control except you. So, again you don't feel up to seeing other people. All this compounds the feelings of loneliness even more.

I believe in taking children with you, so I used to put my baby in a pram and make our way out into society every day, even for just an hour or two. It was healthy to get out of the house, talk to other people and just get used to doing it with a baby in tow.'

— Vanessa (29), mum to Benjamin (one)

The good news is you're not alone in your feelings and there are ways to combat a lonely motherhood.

'It's a relief once we realise that others feel similar things, too, and by talking them through, you feel so much better.'

— Fatma (33), mum to Penelope (four) and Aidan (one)

- Spend time with other mums. Rely on existing friendships, new ones or online friendships.

- Talk to others about how you feel. Your health practitioner, a relative, your partner or another mum can all listen to you and provide some support to relieve your anxieties and thoughts.
- Find, and stick to, a daily routine that meets the needs of the baby and you and also gives you time for some adult company.
- Make an effort to get out and about. Some days this will feel impossible, but when you do feel comfortable, it is healthy to go for a walk, do some window shopping, visit someone or meet up with a friend. You come home feeling more inspired and less isolated.
- Keep in contact with people you used to. Even though you won't have the time or the motivation to spend as much time with colleagues or childless friends as you did before, catching up for lunch, email conversations and phone calls will make you still feel part of the loop, so you don't feel too cut off from everything you were used to.
- Make an effort to reconnect with your partner. It's easy to forget about each other during this transition period, but some intimacy, a decent conversation and sharing loving words are all great ways to remember that you are still part of a couple, not just a mother.
- Have some regular time off from being a mother. Arrange a babysitter to relieve you so that you can do other things you enjoy, such as shopping, beauty treatments, catching up with girlfriends, or some quality time with your partner. This will rejuvenate you and keep you feeling in touch with reality outside the home demands.
- Be positive about the future. Just because you are experiencing moments of loneliness now, that doesn't set the precedent for the next few months or for the next child. Now that you know the feeling of loneliness is normal and that there are ways of dealing with it, you will become better at setting yourself up with a routine and attitude that steers you away from those feelings.

Of course, if these feelings of loneliness never seem to go away then it could be a sign of post-natal depression. If you are ever in doubt, speak to your doctor.

How do I handle the guilt that comes with motherhood?

guilt (gɪlt) *n.*

1. The fact of being responsible for the commission of an offence. **2.** *Law* The fact of having been found to have violated a criminal law; legal culpability. **3.** Responsibility for a mistake or error. **4.** Remorseful awareness of having done something wrong. **5.** Self-reproach for supposed inadequacy or wrongdoing. **6.** A state of regret, insufficiency or misconduct mothers experience shortly after labour and beyond.

Okay, so strictly speaking, you might not find that last definition in any dictionary, but it's still pretty accurate! It comes with the territory that you will feel guilty about something shortly after you give birth and then forever after. It doesn't matter if you are a working or stay-at-home mum, married, single, divorced, or if you have one child or ten. We all experience guilt and feel that we are not doing enough for our children, have made a parenting mistake or are 'selfishly' doing something for ourselves.

Fortunately, you don't have to feel like you are failing your child. It is possible to work through these emotions, lighten up, let go of the guilt and embrace being a better and more relaxed parent.

- Tell yourself that you are doing the best you can in every circumstance.
- Give yourself permission to let go of guilty feelings.

- Remember mums aren't the only ones responsible for your child's life. There are fathers, grandparents, teachers, carers, etc. who also play a role.
- Have confidence in the choices you make for your child.

'When my child misbehaves I have been known to use the naughty corner, throw away favourite toys or cancel playdates. I feel sick at the thought of what I have done. I feel guilty for making him cry or for ruining a great social occasion I know he enjoys. But it is important I enforce boundaries and develop respect and manners so that he grows up to be well behaved. So I trust that I am doing the right thing and try not to let the guilt control my life. Better deal with guilt than a spoilt ratbag.'

— Chantelle (35), mum to Matteus (seven) and Dario (four)

- Think about why exactly you feel guilty and decide if you need to change something in your life to alleviate the feelings.
- Make a list of your essential priorities for the health and wellbeing of your family, and if you are addressing these in your life you don't need to feel guilty.
- Share regular quality time with your family, so when you do something for yourself you can trust that your family will not be disadvantaged.
- Forgive yourself for any mistakes you have made in the past, learn from them for the future, then let go and move on.
- Get used to having time for yourself so that it is part of your life, not something you have to feel guilty about or justify.

How should I involve my partner more?

Some dads are hands-on from the very beginning while others believe child-rearing is predominantly the mother's responsibility. Then there are the dads who would love to play a part but don't have the confidence when their partners continually criticise them for 'not doing it right'. If you want your partner involved in the parenting, you have to actively show your support and encouragement.

'My friend refuses to relinquish any control over parenting duties. No one else, not even her husband, is allowed to put the baby to bed or interfere with the baby routine. Her poor husband changed the kid's nappy at 5 a.m. instead of 7 a.m. and he copped an earful. She won't go out to a function unless it is after the baby's bedtime, because she doesn't trust anyone else to put the baby to sleep. I feel sorry for her husband because you can see he just wants to play a part and have a go, but she is being a bit of a gatekeeper.'

— Jozette (30), mum to Carly (one)

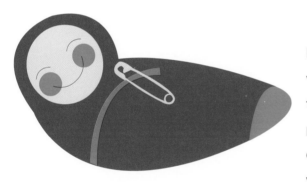

Including the dad more has many benefits. Your partner feels more involved, you get a break and the baby becomes more flexible and better able to handle different parenting styles. Here are some ways you can relinquish some control and involve your partner more:

- Give him set parenting tasks, i.e. bathing, burping or reading stories.
- Make a habit of taking turns doing things.

'I always put our daughter to bed each night. I felt sorry for my husband because he would work long hours and just wanted to relax, so I did it all. But when I fell pregnant I really wanted to just collapse into bed or have a bath by that time of the night and I couldn't do it all. I also wondered how I was going to be able to eventually put two babies to bed. So we made some changes.

My husband started taking her to bed every second night, reading her a story and staying with her until she slept. It was great because not only did I get a night off, but she became less attached to me doing everything and it allowed them to have some quality time together just the two of them.'

— Mataxia (36), mum to Leandra (four) and Mike (one)

- Don't micro-manage — so long as the job gets done, just let him do it his way.
- Schedule regular times for the kids to just be with dad.
- Encourage him and give him the reassurance he needs to feel confident he is doing a great job.

CHAPTER 20

... is for the 'Rewards of motherhood'

As you have heard a thousand times before, motherhood is the hardest job in the world. It's also a thankless and selfless one. From the moment your children are born, you dedicate your heart and soul to them. Their smile lights up your heart, their fart jokes are the funniest things you have ever heard and the smell of their freshly washed hair intoxicates you. It's unbelievable how much love you have for them.

Eighteen years later, they grow up, move to another country and, of course, blame you for a million things you did or did not do. They call you every other month, no longer let you smother them with kisses and cuddles, and are quick to remind you that you are too old to know what is right for their life. Sweet reward that is!

Sometimes, you don't even have to wait eighteen years. Normally, by the time they can talk they are quick to answer back and express how angry they are at you for showing them the naughty corner, making them eat vegetables or for denying them the hundred-dollar toy that just caught their eye. Clearly they don't care that you already purchased 50 million other toys for no good reason, that you spend an hour every night lovingly reading them stories, that you put more effort into their lunch boxes than you did your last business proposal, or that you gave up regular manicures just so they can have fairy dancing classes.

You can't take on the role of mum and expect to one day be rewarded with the words, 'You've done a great job' or 'Thanks for your hard work and sacrifice.' For whatever reason, that might not happen. So relish the role of being a mother for all the great things, lessons and opportunities the *role* offers you, as well as your children.

While our babies are the ultimate reason for our happiness and ability to function, we can't only look to them to make us happy, even if our hearts don't beat quite the same way without them. That's simply putting too much pressure on them. Naturally, they will always be our major source of happiness and inspiration, but there are many other rewards of motherhood.

Here are ten significant ways in which motherhood will reward you mentally, physically and emotionally, allowing you to strengthen and develop your mind, body and attitude. If you ever have a frustrating day, or need to put things in perspective, consider these perks of the job.

1. A greater respect and love for your body.
2. A deeper feeling of love.
3. You wake up feeling lucky every day.
4. Closer ties to your partner.
5. Understanding your values in life.
6. New career perspective.
7. More in tune with world issues.
8. A less selfish existence.

9. Closer to family.

10. Healthier lifestyle.

A greater respect and love for your body

'Somebody asked me if I am happy with my body after giving birth. I am flabbier, still carrying extra weight and have now got uneven breasts. But I am happier. This body managed to bring a miracle into my life. I have so much more respect for it now, because of this. Stuff the extra kilos. My body should be worshipped for everything it has been through.'

— Victoria (33), mum to Jamie (seven) and Erik, Ethan and Noah (three)

You should be congratulated for what you have put your body through. All those years pre-baby you slaved away at the gym, forced your way into skinny jeans, tried the latest fad diet and purchased every anti-cellulite cream on the market. You did this to look good and feel great about your body.

Then you got pregnant and all the work you'd done over the years went down the gurgler. In pregnancy you put up with dark stretch marks, back fat and 20 unnecessary kilos. Post-baby you have excess stomach skin, wider hips, a thicker waist and more stubborn back fat. Not to mention zero time to slave away at the gym or a spare $200 for creams and diet shakes. Yet this is a very small price to pay for what you get in return, isn't it?

You have a golden excuse to look at your body with a less critical eye. Now is the time to embrace the beauty of your body and love it for what it is and what it has been able to do for another human being. So long as you are healthy, does it really matter that much if you are carrying extra padding here and there, if you can't wear the same clothes you did when you were at university or that your thighs keep wobbling long after you stop moving?

Rather than criticising the individual parts we all have, start looking at your body as a whole. At the end of the day, your body is a miracle maker and the ultimate source of comfort and security for your child. Now is the time to wear with pride those bathers with built-in tummy suction. You have the best excuse in the world.

A deeper feeling of love

'The love I have for my babies is out of this world. It really is like watching somebody walking around with your heart in their hands. You love them so much it hurts. Some days you think you are the only person in the world with so much love to give. But most parents are the same.'

— Logan (38), mum to Kirrily (seven), Caleb (four) and Ryan (one)

Of course people who do not have children experience love. Love for their partners, love for their pets, love for friends and relatives, and love for life. Having said that, most parents have experienced love pre-baby and post-baby and comment that the love you feel once you have a child is different to the kind of love you experience from other sources in life.

Without being too soppy, the love you feel for your child is an emotion that makes you treasure another individual so wholly, unconditionally and selflessly that you would never have believed it possible if you hadn't experienced it for yourself. This child can melt your insides with a hug, a toothless kiss and a squeal, and makes every day sacred. This is pretty powerful stuff! Not everybody has this kind of love in their lives.

'You see, there's love, and there's love. My toddler can wake me up with the softest kiss and pat on my head and I will jump out of bed and make her breakfast each day. But if my husband comes too close to me in the morning I have to tell him to go brush his teeth and get his own breakfast!'

— Mischa (31), mum to Ruby (two)

You wake up feeling lucky every day

Some people spend years and their entire superannuation fund trying to fall pregnant and have a child, with no success. Others had a child who was sadly taken away much too soon. And here you are reading this book because you are one of the lucky ones blessed with a miracle who stares back at you with trust, love and innocence.

You can't take this kind of luck for granted. How many people receive the daily pleasure of listening to squealing laughter, feel skin as soft as silk, or receive a lightning bolt smile just for walking into a room? We have someone who makes us forget about troubles at work with one enthusiastic cuddle; makes a long, lonely drive home one full of anticipation; and believes we have what it takes to make the world a better place. This is all yours.

'I have two treasures who are all mine. I can't believe it some days. I get to watch them grow, learn, experience and know I played a key part in all this as well as their happiness along the way. Because of them I also get to grow, learn and experience. This is a privilege not everybody shares.'

— Lexie (33), mum to Spencer (four) and Archie (two)

Closer ties to your partner

There may be moments when you feel your relationship is being tested. As you are both learning how to adjust to caring for a child, surviving on limited sleep and handling an increased amount of responsibility, you might start stressing out more than you did when you renovated the house or planned the wedding. All this can cause some tension and arguments between you.

Fortunately, as you adjust, you will start working more in unison. You become less tired, more experienced and can communicate more rationally. Before long, the transition has been made and you feel closer than ever. This child has created an unbreakable, permanent bond between the two of you. You have each other to thank for him or her.

Many women agree that you form a stronger emotional connection to your partner after having a child. Previously, you worked on your marriage together while you each had your own individual needs and career responsibilities. But now it is no longer just the two of you chasing your own dreams and interests. You are a family now and experience a shared sense of responsibility. This takes your marriage to a whole new level and brings you closer to one another.

Understanding your values in life

After giving birth, it doesn't take long to realise that you don't have the time or motivation to do everything you did before or planned to do now. Your time and energy are more precious than ever and you have more than enough demands on your plate to know that any unnecessary jobs will tip you over the edge.

As you accept that you can't be responsible for everything, you start to think very carefully about what it is you want most in your life. Motherhood provides the perfect excuse to sort through different factors and focus on what truly matters. This is what will give you the most satisfaction and fulfilment in life. Everything else will just wear you down unnecessarily.

It's a great lesson. You quickly figure out what gives you the most pleasure in life and alter your priorities to suit. You no longer find yourself spending time with people who aren't important to you or doing things you don't really want to do. Instead you spend quality time on the relationships that are most rewarding and doing things that satisfy your priorities and make you happy.

New career perspective

After adjusting to your new self and realising that your identity is not linked to your work, you return to work with a new, refreshing attitude. You have seen what else matters in life, you appreciate the need for balance and you know not to sweat the small stuff. So now you focus more on the bigger picture and care far less about irrelevant office politics.

Being a mother will bring you closer to other employees, co-workers or clients who have children and help you bond professionally. This can be a great thing in business as you can naturally relate to people on a new level. You are also a lot more understanding and flexible with other parents in the workforce. People will recognise and appreciate this attitude.

Motherhood has taught you a lot about time management and organisational skills; this makes you an asset to any employer. You know firsthand how to juggle more than one thing and can maximise your time better than before. You work faster and smarter.

Even though you have a greater need for flexible work conditions, overall you are more productive, have stronger professional relationships and can focus more clearly on the key objectives of your role. This makes you a valuable asset.

More in tune with world issues

Pre-baby, how much thought did you really give to government health reforms, medical services in other countries, pesticides in vegetables, child flu vaccine warnings or changes to gun regulations? It's likely you put more thought into what you would make for dinner, who to catch up with over the weekend and where you should holiday next. Things are different now. Community issues are more significant because now they impact on your life.

Now you suddenly have deep feelings and opinions about things you were previously indifferent to. (For the same reason, you also cry at soppy commercials featuring the puppy that gives the toilet paper to its owner — but that's another story.) You pay attention to what is happening around you because you want to have a better understanding of how it will affect your children and your children's children. You want to be more involved to ensure that no tragedies or health crises impact your life.

As a mother, you have more interest in and knowledge about what is going on around you. You care more about your environment and have compassion for different community groups. This makes you more in touch with world affairs and, hopefully, a stronger advocate for issues that matter.

A less selfish existence

Not many mothers remember the life they enjoyed before the baby came along. Others look back on their fond memories as if they were a dream. All that time, money and energy dedicated to making you and only you happy! Do you remember the holidays, the expensive clothes, taking two hours to get ready, the full social life, and completing the washing in one load a fortnight?

Now you are on call 24/7 for the rest of your life. You are responsible for someone else's life and needs. While it seems daunting, it is the ultimate way to develop and grow as a more responsible and balanced individual who cares more for others than themselves.

You are no longer the only one who matters. In fact, someone else matters *more*. While you can and should still find a way to live a life that you enjoy, it will now be built around the needs of your child. It's amazing that you can change your life so dramatically, altering your dreams and aspirations to better suit your child, yet still find so much personal fulfilment and happiness.

'I no longer think about the sacrifices that came with motherhood. I've done it all and I genuinely enjoyed it at the time. I wouldn't change it for the world.'

— Monique (23), mum to Veronica (two)

Closer to family

'It was only after I had children of my own that I realised how much my parents loved me. I completely underestimated it.'

— Lillian (32), mum to Callam (four) and Xavier (one)

Once you have a baby, don't be surprised if you start to love your parents differently. You may also start to feel closer to them now than you ever did growing up. You quickly realise the enormity of what they sacrificed to give you the life you had. You feel the pain you must have caused them with your teenage angst and rebellious activities. Even if they did things you did not agree with, now you understand on a completely different level that they did everything for you, with pure love, and it was their way of doing the right thing.

Having a baby can also help you bond with family members you probably didn't expect to. You can become closer to aunts, grandmothers, cousins and even mothers-in-law. You feel more emotionally connected because you have all been through the same thing. There is a greater respect and empathy for these women because you all know what a huge responsibility it is to raise children and what a difficult, commendable task it is to bring well-adjusted, good kids into this world.

Hopefully, the experience of having a child will give you more patience, time and respect for your mum and other relatives so that you develop a special and healthy appreciation for what you each had to and have to go though. This will help you bond and make your relationship stronger.

Healthier lifestyle

Being the responsible, new parent that you are, it's likely that pregnancy and breastfeeding made you carefully re-evaluate your diet, exercise and lifestyle. You stopped drinking, taking drugs, smoking and over-indulging in foods your body did not need. You took vitamins, kept up your fluids and rested when you could.

'I used to have the occasional social cigarette. But now that my child is getting older and watches what I do, I recognise it is a bad habit I don't want her to get into. I realise that I am a role model and have to stop immediately.'

— Madison (34), mum to Bethany (three) and Toby (one)

Now that you are a parent, hopefully you have the motivation to keep up some of those habits for the long term, instead of going back to takeaway most nights, or too much chocolate, wine and cigarettes. Experts say that children learn more from you by watching than they do from listening to what you tell them. So you really need to stand by the values you want them to adopt.

If you want them to learn healthy habits, then you need to do more than just tell them to eat their vegetables, ride their bike, go to sleep or drink their milk. To make an impact and see results, you need to adopt and enforce healthy lifestyle habits for yourself. If they see that healthy living and healthy eating are a way of life, then that is what they will be accustomed to. Before you know it, motherhood will have given you the perfect opportunity to live a healthier life that benefits both you and your family.

CHAPTER 21

S

... is for 'Self-esteem'

The content in this chapter works in unison with the content in Chapter 5 on 'Confidence building'. Self-esteem and confidence are different but complementary. You can have one without the other, but when you have both of these attributes you can achieve great things for yourself and your family. By addressing your self-esteem and your confidence, you will have the strength, drive, motivation and belief in yourself and your ability to succeed at whatever is important to you.

This chapter looks at the importance of self-esteem and how it influences your role as a mum and a person. You will also discover numerous ways to build self-esteem, even if you have had issues with it in the past. This way you can easily adopt the right attitude and have the self-respect to love yourself for who you are.

'When my baby cries or won't settle, I feel like I am not good at what I do and that I am a bad mother. I wish I could believe in myself a little more and trust that I am actually a good mother doing the best she can.'

— Erika (34), mum to Donovan (one)

'There are times when I feel stupid when I catch up with other mums who are working. They all have something interesting to say but I'm just a stay-at-home mum. This makes me feel like I am not as smart. I don't respect myself as much as I did and as much as I should.'

— Pamela (36), mum to Jason (four) and Chris (one)

Self-esteem is the personal opinion you have of yourself, whether you think you are important, and how much you accept, value, believe and respect yourself. Confidence, on the other hand, means that you trust what you are capable of. It is confidence that makes you feel certain you can set goals and actually achieve them. To put it simply, self-esteem is about how you view *who you are*, while confidence is about how you view *what you can do*.

We start to develop our self-esteem from a very young age. It's something that is influenced by our surroundings, how well we succeed at school and in social environments and, most importantly, the messages we receive from the people who surround us. If you have grown up with positive influences and experiences, it is more likely you will have a higher self-esteem as a mum and will be able to interact more positively with the world in your new circumstances. You naturally feel good about yourself and demonstrate self-respect as you learn the ropes of parenting and adjusting to being a mum while remaining an individual.

On the flip side, if in the past you have been strongly criticised, ridiculed or made to feel inferior or incapable, you may have developed low self-esteem. This, in turn, can make you vulnerable to negativity. For no good reason, you may doubt your self-worth and how good a mother and person you really are. This then makes you feel insecure with relationships (such as a relationship with a partner or new baby) and leads to an overall lack of confidence. In some instances, low self-esteem can also trigger depression.

As a new mum, facing new challenges, dreams and issues, having a higher self-esteem will give you a positive attitude towards how you treat and value yourself during this time. A healthy self-esteem will carry you through the bad days and keep you feeling good about yourself. While the occasional moment of doubt may briefly threaten the opinion you have of yourself, in your heart you will know that you are a reliable, hard-working, capable mum and person, able to make the right decisions for yourself and your baby.

If breastfeeding, settling or a new routine isn't working out as you thought, it doesn't mean you are a failure. You are still as wonderful and smart and worthy of a bright future as you were before you had to deal with these changes. You just need to deal with and move past circumstances that affect your attitude and personal opinion and continue to focus on the great things about you and what you *are* doing. This will give you the strength to keep progressing positively.

'I really did not enjoy breastfeeding at all, but the books I read and professionals I spoke with continued to advocate how much better it was for the baby, so even if I wanted to stop, I felt too guilty.

I struggled to express, which meant I could never leave her in someone else's care so I could have a well-earned break. This loss of freedom depressed me sometimes when I couldn't go to the gym or have a massage or a simple dinner with a friend. I really believed that I would be a selfish mother if I stopped.

But after breastfeeding for three months I had to stop. I was desperate for some time out so that I could work on my "self".

This did not make me a bad person. I trusted my decision and knew that I am now actually a better mum and a happier person to be around.'

— Meagan (32), mum to Tilly (one)

It's only human to make mistakes and sometimes doubt what you are doing and where you are going. But if you genuinely believe in yourself, your ongoing attitude will reflect that and give you the strength to trust your decisions as you figure it all out. In turn, you will be happier with yourself, more motivated and have the right attitude to be the best mum and person you can be.

How mothers benefit from a healthy self-esteem

- It directly affects your behaviour.
- It can affect your thinking so that you have a more positive attitude.
- It influences how you relate to other people.
- It affects the opinion you have of yourself and self-worth.
- A lack of self-esteem can interfere with success.
- It equips you for facing challenges.
- It has a direct bearing on your happiness, wellbeing and optimism.
- It can give you confidence.
- It encourages you to love yourself for who you are.
- It gives you courage to chase your dreams and be the woman you want to be.

As a mum, it is important to be aware of low self-esteem and try to combat those feelings. In this way, you will have all the tools in place to live a healthy, positive life and show respect for yourself in the process. If you have suffered from low self-esteem in the past, there are ways you can re-learn what you think of yourself. And even if you have always had positive self-esteem, you might find it needs some fine-tuning as you deal with the totally new journey ahead of you.

I have included twenty different techniques to assist in the process of developing your self-esteem. Identify what approach would work best for you and aim to focus on it daily. Make it part of your life and attitude until you honestly believe in yourself and recognise your value and potential as a woman, mother and individual.

Twenty tactics for building self-esteem

1. Start step by step. Decide what part of your self-esteem needs work and focus on one change at a time before making another change. For example, you might want to develop your self-esteem in terms of how you view yourself as a parent. Or you might want to work on how you view your self-worth now that you are no longer in the workforce.

2. Feel good about yourself today. Don't think, 'When I have done this, or achieved that, then I will feel proud of myself and be happy.' Appreciate yourself in the now.

3. Be proactive in finding and voicing what it is you need to feel good about yourself. It might be that you need a buddy to depend on when you are feeling down, to prop you up and remind you how special you are.

4. Accept responsibility for your own happiness. Don't let other people define who you are or what your dreams should be.

5. Try to improve yourself for you, not to compete with another mum or person.

6. Learn something new. The sense of accomplishment and stimulation will make you feel good about yourself.

7. Trust yourself. If you have to make a decision and feel uncertain, just remind yourself of the positives that could happen and move forwards feeling good.

8. Spend more time with positive people so that they influence you and make you feel more positive as well.

9. Give yourself a reward for doing well or when you feel a sense of accomplishment.

10. Don't listen to negative comments or thoughts that can damage your self-esteem. This will set you back as you work on the positive feelings you have about yourself.

11. Focus more on the messages you hear or tell yourself that contribute to your positive self-esteem and self-worth.

12. Repeat positive affirmations about yourself regularly.

13. If somebody says something negative to you, don't take it personally. Some people feel better about themselves when they put others down. Instead remind yourself why their comments can't possibly be true or think about how the comment could be viewed as constructive criticism from which you can learn.

14. Whenever you hear yourself saying something negative either to yourself or others, re-word it so that the talk is focused on the positive.

15. Let go of the guilty feelings as guilt can hold you back from having a positive self-esteem. You are still a worthy mum and individual if you have regular time out or decide to stop breastfeeding.

16. If you have done something wrong, assume responsibility then move forward. Don't dwell on negative experiences as the feelings will drag you down.

17. Do more exercise that you enjoy. Exercise boosts self-esteem as it refreshes your mind, gives you more energy and improves your body image.

18. Love yourself for who you are and for the special characteristics you have instead of focusing on what you don't have, or how you think you don't measure up.

19. Find some regular quiet time to reconnect with your thoughts and to make sure you are still feeling positive about yourself, what you are doing and where you are going.

20. Learn to laugh more. Rather than dwelling on self-pity, learn to laugh about things or at least lighten the mood. Otherwise you will just feel sorry for yourself and even more insecure.

With a positive, healthy self-esteem you can live a happier life and truly feel proud of yourself. By recognising and valuing your self-importance you show respect for yourself. You set an example for your children and for others around you and communicate that 'you're worth it' and deserve to feel good about yourself and live the life you desire.

CHAPTER 22

... is for 'Tips from other mothers'

'It's always after we hit rock bottom and experience the ultimate meltdown that we finally figure things out. Only then does everything click into place and make more sense.'

— Nina (40), mum to Elliot and Angus (two)

The dramatic toll having a baby takes on your mind, body and life is truly incredible, especially in the early weeks, months and, some would argue, years. For many new mums, it feels as if there is just no light at the end of the tunnel. You genuinely believe you will be living Groundhog Day, forever. This is despite well-meaning advice from others and their assurances that life apparently will get easier.

Fortunately, our sisters have proven to us that even if you are left on your own to work things out, you will eventually make sense of your new life, mind, body and attitude. However, if you *are* on your own, it will take longer than you might imagine as you learn all the key lessons five minutes too late!

Speak to other mothers and you quickly learn that they each have their own gem of advice that personally saved them from going insane. Here we have compiled the most common tips and words of wisdom that mums share with the new mothers entering the jungle of parenthood. This chapter will save you much time, energy, heartache and unnecessary grey hairs.

Become a time-management master

Newborn demands, household chores, other kids, a husband and perhaps even work will drain every minute of your day. It's like living on a rollercoaster. Days turn into nights and weeks turn into months before you notice you still haven't had time to book in a wax or hair appointment, let alone some quiet time to see a movie or catch up with a friend.

If you commit to some basic time-management rules, you will create more time for your family and partner and even gain some coveted 'me' time.

'To survive, I suggest you get organised, delegate, multitask, say no, be flexible, have a routine, prioritise, use time-management tools to help, devise an action plan, don't take on too much and take shortcuts where you can.'

— Joan (34), mum to Michaelangelo (four) and Oliver (one)

Put your needs first

Initially, the idea of taking care of yourself seems far-fetched and impossible, especially if you don't have help or a textbook baby who gives you a chance to have a shower without interruption. But you have to nourish your own heath and wellbeing before you can take care of everyone and everything else.

For example, have a 15-minute rest before doing four loads of washing, eat a meal before cleaning the breakfast dishes, and slip into a hot nightly bath before putting away all of the toys left out during the day. This way your mind and body are ready and able to handle the next round, which is most likely in a few hours' time when you have to get up for the nightly feeds. It is easy to miss your only window of opportunity!

'If you don't put your needs first and sleep when you can, eat properly and address other areas of your life that crave attention, you will slowly crash and burn. Then you are no good to anyone! I find a regular break to take care of you will actually make you a better mother.'

— Jenna (36), mum to Adran (two)

Keep your priorities in check

Decide what you really want to achieve for the day, week and month. It should be a combination of what *must* get done so that you and your family can function and a range of other things you would *like* to find time for. By mixing these two types of demands you can feel happy and confident that you are achieving what really matters in your life. The trick is not to be distracted or neglect the things you would like to find time for and focus too much on the 'must do' items. By mixing the two you will have balance, a sense of purpose and a feeling of satisfaction. If you stay focused on priorities you will feel like you are getting what you want out of life.

'I used to put ironing before sex, dishes before coffee and gardening before entertaining. I finally realised that by doing this I was missing out on sacred time with my partner, friends and myself; three things that I relish in life. It took some time to realise that it's not the end of the world if the house isn't looking spotless 100 per cent of the time.'

— Maxine (29), mum to Eve (one)

Be realistic about life

Before having a child, you may have assumed having a new life in the house would be easy enough. You expected to juggle a baby with a home business, domestic chores and quality time with your partner. You probably thought you could even maintain your busy social life and independence by simply expressing milk. But life doesn't always work out as we think. A business can demand more time than a newborn to be successful, there is more housework than you realised, and your baby won't take the bottle and simply refuses to sleep during the day.

If this is your life, don't try to set unrealistic demands and expectations that you are not currently equipped to handle. Take the time to accept your new life, both the good and the not so good. Deal with life as you know it instead of stressfully trying to accommodate what is clearly not possible. Once you adjust to life's new demands and routine, it won't be long before you wake up and recognise you can reclaim a version of your previous life. You will once again have the ability, time, flexibility and freedom to do more of what you want to do.

'I wanted to work from home immediately, because I thought I would be bored. My first child was always sleeping, so I was shocked when this one woke up continuously during the night and struggled to settle during the day for more than a 30-minute catnap. This left me with no time to work.

I was so tired I could barely string together a sentence, let alone work professionally. So I had to cancel work commitments for a few months to focus on being a mum — just until the little one established a more predictable routine and I was confident I could handle speaking to adults again.

Once I accepted that I wasn't fit to work yet, a pressure lifted off me. I felt more relaxed and enjoyed the next three months adjusting to sleep deprivation, getting to know my baby and establishing a routine that prepared me for work instead of trying to do it all when I really couldn't.'

— Teagan (36), mum to Tamara (four) and Emma (two)

Live up to your expectations, not somebody else's

It is easy to get caught up trying to be the mum you think you should be, rather than the mum you really want to be. You can be distracted by the celebrity mums you see in the media, how your close friends are mothering, or by memories of how you were mothered as a child. But you can't try to be someone you are not.

Work out what your definition of a great mum is and work towards being that mum. Your child might not be dressed in the latest designer gear, have private baby yoga lessons from three months or listen to Mozart every nap time. But what you can provide is someone who is accessible, nurturing and gives unconditional love and support. Isn't that most important?

'A lot of mums start mothering by doing everything the experts say you should do, but find it is impossible to keep up and do everything by the book. So they end up modifying parenting to suit their personality and abilities.

So what if the baby misses out on tummy time every wake time, or that you read them a glossy magazine instead of a picture book? You're still a fabulous, award-worthy mum if you can provide a soft place for them to fall and if you're both clean, fed and content most of the time.'

— Sarita (35), mum to Bella-Grace (two)

Don't be a control freak

If you try to control everything in your surroundings you will just make life that much more stressful for yourself and those around you. It is really hard, and at times impossible, to control everything when you are juggling a new baby and rampant hormones. You might need to let others help with the housework, even if it is not to your liking. You might need to give your partner the chance to bathe, settle and put the baby to sleep so you can have a rest, even if he doesn't quite know how to wrap the baby the way you do. You might need to pull back on work commitments so you can sleep. And you might need to live with eating leftovers three nights in a row, if it means giving you and your partner more time to reconnect. Let a few things go in order to be at peace with yourself and life.

'For now, don't worry so much about everything being perfect. You have the rest of your life to be a control freak. Sure, it's not a perfect scenario, but by letting go of trying to control certain aspects, you will not feel so disappointed with yourself and your life when you realise you can't do the impossible. Nobody can — at least not in the beginning, or without a nanny, housekeeper and chef to help.'

— Magdalena (28), mum to Ricky (three)

Take pride in your appearance

When you make the effort to look better, you feel better and act more confident. Employ some self-respect instead of saying, 'It's too hard!' or that you 'never go anywhere anyway' to warrant the effort. You're still a woman as well as a mum, so you shouldn't stop taking care of your appearance. Clean yourself up, make the effort for yourself the way you used to and stop the self-neglect. If your partner or children (when they grow up) stop taking pride in their appearance you would be disappointed that they stopped valuing themselves. Set an example.

'I used to complain that my husband no longer made an effort to look good for me. Then I had a good look at myself in the mirror. I had to admit that my unshaved legs, tattered pyjamas and a hairy chin didn't exactly spell "sexy mama". So I bought some decent, semi-sexy (but still practical) sleepwear and a new razor. I'm not quite as foxy as I used to be, but it is a step in the right direction at least!'

— Vicky (37), mum to Natasha (six) and Corina (two)

Nurture your relationship with your partner

The introduction of a child is a big change for both parents. Previously, you had similar daily routines, mirrored career ambitions and funny workplace stories to share over dinner. You were best friends. Now, you are too busy being a mum and dad, have a totally different routine to one another, rarely share dinner and your career ambitions are completely different. You can easily lose some commonality because of this and find you have less time and energy for each other.

Therefore, in order to maintain a strong, healthy relationship, and have something to talk about when the children leave home, it is more important than ever to keep connected and in touch with each other as people, not just as parents, amidst the hustle, stress and routine of family life. This takes time and effort.

'I always have the best of intentions to have a glass of wine and deep and meaningful chat with my husband when he gets home from work. But by that time I am too tired to talk to anyone. There is nothing left of me. So to make up for lost time during the week, we all get out of the house on the weekend, with the baby, away from the routine, unmade beds, paperwork to finish, etc.

By getting away from it all, even just for a coffee, we can actually unwind and chat. Otherwise we just find ourselves at opposite ends of the house doing our own thing, once again, not talking.'

— Cara (33), mum to Aalijah (five) and Matthew (three)

Have a passion

Your individual passions are important because they shape who you are as a person, make you feel more like yourself and give you that personal sense of pride and satisfaction. So give yourself a reason to have some fire in your belly. Identify something, aside from the role of mother, that you really love doing and make room for it in your life. There are ways to make it work for everyone in the family so you don't feel like you are neglecting those around you when you devote some time to yourself.

'I need to do something for me otherwise I feel resentful. I love my family to death but my lifestyle as a taxi driver, maid, cook and everything else gets mundane. Regardless of how tired I am, I need a break from it all to remind myself that I am an individual with individual needs and interests as well. I've recently started tap dancing of all things!'

— Lily (37), mum to Logan (six) and Zac and Benjamin (two)

Get out of the house every day

After being stuck in the house all day, hearing the word 'Mum' a hundred times before lunch and watching the dishes and washing pile up before your eyes, you will be amazed how quickly fresh air can calm you down, clear your head and help you refocus on the next round. Whether you get some fresh air on your own or with the family, you still benefit by stepping away from surroundings that have a tendency to close up on you sometimes.

'I have to get out of the house every day. Even if it is cold I will rug up and throw an extra blanket on the baby and go for a walk. It's the only thing that keeps me sane.'

— Vienna (31), mum to Toby (one)

Talk to someone when you are feeling down

Too many mums are scared to open up to friends or a professional practitioner and say that they are not coping for fear of being judged a failure. Many want to appear like they have it all together, or think they can sort it out on their own. But keeping feelings bottled up does more harm than good, so it is helpful to speak up when there are serious factors bothering you.

It is not a crime to admit that your marriage is suffering because you don't have the time or energy for your husband. You are not failing if you admit that sometimes you would rather do housework than read yet another story to your child. And you are not the only one who gets anxious being around other women or feels isolated being at home. Learn to break through these barriers and speak up. You will be surprised how many other women share these feelings. There are ways to help you overcome them.

'The more I started confiding to other women about some of the issues I was experiencing, the more I discovered that they too had a similar experience. Talking made me feel more "normal" and lightened my mood.'

— Erini (36), mum to Clarisse (four) and Monika (one)

Learn to appreciate the little things in life

After years spent chasing promotions, more money and gruelling ambitions, having a baby will introduce a different kind of pleasure: one derived from the little things in life. Pre-kids, how many times did you stop to pick flowers, feed ducks, watch a butterfly or just sit on the grass and have a picnic? Yes, it does sound corny, but you will be doing these things a lot more than you did in the past. Surprisingly, the simple things we take for granted can relax you, inspire you and provide a break from the serious side of life that's responsible for our wrinkles and greying hair. They give us a chance to refocus on other parts of life and come back down to earth.

'Sharing simple experiences with my child actually gives me a lot of pleasure too and puts life into perspective for me.'

— Soloma (37), mum to Dinesh (three) and Seema (one)

Let go of the guilt

It's too easy to feel guilty about anything and everything. You feel guilty for working, for not working, for not doing enough around the home, for making the beds instead of reading stories, for serving takeaway instead of cooking and for indulging in something you enjoy instead of being a hands-on 'mum' 100 per cent of the time. The guilt is never-ending but you have to learn to let it go so that you can live real life.

'If I let guilt get in the way of making decisions such as sending my kids to childcare, choosing a government school instead of private and using sweets as a bribe, I would have become a basket case in no time.'

— Lorna (36), mum to Gavin (seven) and Luke (four)

CHAPTER 23

... is for 'Underdogs who inspire'

'Train like an underdog, win like a champion.'

— Rockafella Family

As you enter motherhood you sometimes feel a part of yourself slipping away. Not intentionally, but that's just how things sometimes work out. Even if you want to hold on to your sense of self, there is either no time or you don't want to sacrifice the tiny bit of spare time you do have to follow your personal aspirations. You are just too busy changing nappies, singing nursery rhymes, ironing, soaking clothes, mashing bananas and squeezing your pelvic floor muscles (does anybody really do them, I wonder?). After a while you soon forget how good it feels to do what you love and no longer bother with your needs. A million other things come first.

It doesn't have to be this way. Here are the stories of six inspiring women who all have something in common: they are celebrating a successful passion they found time for *after* they became mothers, and each of them was an underdog.

Read their profiles to familiarise yourself with their traits. They are proof that, even with children, you can realise your dreams — if you really want to. Now is as good a time as any to change your life for the better. Sure, having children does make your life impossibly busy, but as these women demonstrate, you have every chance of reaching your potential to become the person you want to be and live a life you really want.

Like these mums, you can make the decision and the commitment to be in the driver's seat. You can be an active participant in your life, rather than living day in and day out doing the same old thing. Now is the time to be excited about what you want and can achieve.

Suburban mum becomes international inventor: Mary Toniolo

Mary Toniolo is a 50-something, typical mother of two, based in Melbourne, Australia.

She had the idea to create a home ballet studio for her daughter so that she could learn ballet at home instead of in the competitive classroom environment. Mary recognised that the product, made with Velcro and carpet, could actually be a prototype for something much bigger. After fine-tuning the idea further by producing an accompanying instructional DVD, developing proper moulds and including professional artwork, Bella Dancerella was born.

Bella Dancerella was featured at the New York Toy Trade Fair and ended up winning the top international prize, the coveted 2005 Toy of the Year award, beating the likes of Mattel and Fisher-Price at their own game. In 2005, Mary Toniolo put herself on the map when she became one of the first small businesses ever to beat the odds and win this award. Since then, Bella Dancerella has achieved global recognition and sold millions of products around the world.

Mary has further developed the brand to include other titles and accessories. The next instalment is to make it an Australian television program. Not bad going for a typical, suburban mum who recognised an opportunity and went for it.

WHAT MAKES HER AN UNDERDOG?

- She came from a difficult background where, as the eldest of six children, she was largely responsible for home life.
- She had to deal with an early failed marriage.
- She grew up being told she was incapable of doing anything.
- As an adult she had no career aspirations.
- Originally her idea was scoffed at and rejected by distributors before a major distributor finally backed it.
- She had an unsuccessful first go at the New York Toy Trade Fair before she actually won the award and changed her life forever.

LESSONS WE CAN LEARN FROM THIS MOTHER

- If you apply yourself you can do anything.
- Learn to recognise opportunity.
- Get professional business support.
- Don't be daunted by challenges and setbacks.
- If you recognise a need in the marketplace, follow your instincts and have a go.

HER TRAITS

- Planner
- Confident
- Innovative

- Persistent
- Resilient
- Practical
- Resourceful
- Committed

HER LIGHT-BULB MOMENT

It was practicality that ignited Mary's invention and changed her destiny. Mary wanted to create a fun dance space for her daughter so that she could enjoy herself away from the strict expectations and seriousness of formal dance lessons. As she was developing the concept, she truly believed that it had the potential to excite ballet enthusiasts everywhere.

Home cook launches new life as celebrity chef: Julie Goodwin

Julie Goodwin is clearly a family woman at heart who simply loves to cook for the people close to her. The 40-year-old from the NSW Central Coast is a mother of three boys, a wife and businesswoman. Until recently, Julie worked with her husband in their IT business. While she is proud of her life and business, it is cooking that has always been her passion, as she genuinely relishes bringing people together over a delectable meal. Julie has long harboured a dream to open up her own restaurant.

This mother of all cooks took ten steps closer to realising her dream and beyond, when she entered a reality television cooking show and dazzled television officials with her hearty home-style cooking. Her potential was instantly recognised. She went on to beat 7000 cooking hopefuls and secured her place in the top twenty contestants of the show.

Week after week, she continued to exploit her talents as a fabulous, capable cook and won the title. Not only did she win a monetary prize but she also won a new life. Julie Goodwin has since released a cookbook, has her own television cooking show, is a brand ambassador for food-related products and is a credible industry spokesperson.

She is living the life she dreamed of and is an inspiration to mothers everywhere who slave away in the kitchen, making delicious meals for those they love. Julie proves that everything is possible for the ordinary, everyday, hard-working mum.

WHAT MAKES HER AN UNDERDOG?

- She is a self-confessed 'home cook', not an internationally renowned chef.
- Julie is just an ordinary mum who did something extraordinary for herself.
- She admits that the journey to the end was really, really hard and one that made her question if she genuinely had what it takes to succeed.

LESSONS WE CAN LEARN FROM THIS MOTHER

- Make the most of your own abilities.
- Fight for what you really want.
- Keep going when you experience setbacks.
- You should follow your dream.
- Have a go.
- Sometimes sacrifices are necessary.

HER TRAITS

- Humble
- Honest
- Persistent
- Tenacious
- Hard working

HER LIGHT-BULB MOMENT

Julie Goodwin took the first step to changing her destiny when she made the decision to apply as a contestant on an upcoming reality television show. She stopped dreaming about how great it would be to make a living out of cooking and actually had a go at realising her potential.

Weight-loss wonder woman helps thousands globally: Karen Gatt

How many times a week do you visit your trusty clothesline? With a newborn in tow it is probably quite a few. Did you ever think it could hold the secret to shedding the extra pregnancy weight you still can't lose? For Karen Gatt, the clothesline was instrumental in changing her life for good.

At 26 years of age and weighing 136 kilograms, Karen Gatt was disgusted with what she saw in the mirror and fed up with watching her life pass her by. She was dangerously overweight but with two toddlers to look after and virtually non-existent self-esteem, this everyday mum couldn't even handle going for a walk in public. She was too embarrassed and fearful of being ridiculed. After failing yet another weight-loss program, she planned her own simple eating plan accompanied by regular walks around the clothesline.

A year later, Karen had lost an impressive 70 kilos and gained her life and self-worth back. She has kept the weight off for over ten years as she relentlessly helps others in similar circumstances to believe in themselves. This weight-loss queen is an inspiration for mothers who are depressed, feel hopeless and are isolating themselves from life.

Karen is proud of the new woman she has become and continues to transform lives. She now runs boot camps, gym sessions, support groups, a website, has written numerous books and is preparing for her assault on the United States. She is a very real woman with a very real success story. If she can do it, you can do it.

WHAT MAKES HER AN UNDERDOG?

- Karen had always been overweight, ever since she was a child.
- She was ridiculed for her weight as she was growing up.
- She endured emotional and physical pain and suffering as a result of her weight.
- She hated herself for 26 years and struggled to even look at herself in the mirror.
- She was eating herself to death.
- She could barely walk to the letterbox or actively play with her children.

LESSONS WE CAN LEARN FROM THIS MOTHER

- Fight for that dream because the dream is just around the corner.
- If you want success you have to get up and make it happen.
- You can't share love with anyone else if you hate yourself.
- Your life is what you make of it.
- All it takes is one step forward to change your life.

HER TRAITS

- Tough
- Generous
- Practical
- Warm
- Friendly
- Supportive
- Motivational
- Honest

HER LIGHT-BULB MOMENT

At a Mother's Day family function, Karen watched enviously as other beautiful mothers danced and appeared to be enjoying a life she wasn't actively participating in. That's the moment she finally found the strength and the courage to resolve what was holding her back from enjoying her own life. She realised that she deserved better and from that point on everything changed.

Philanthropist creates national charitable foundation: Rachel Stanfield-Porter

When Melbourne-based philanthropist Rachel Stanfield-Porter lost two babies to miscarriage and stillbirth, she was inconsolable and struggled to find an outlet where she could talk and grieve and deal with the pain. At the time, nobody really knew how to comfort bereaved parents.

After she had given birth to one healthy boy and was pregnant with her second, she decided to help families dealing with such tragic loss and set up Bonnie Babes. Bonnie Babes is now a globally recognised support network set up to assist around 20,000 families per annum deal with losing a child via stillbirth or miscarriage.

From her lounge room, this remarkable mum organically started and developed an amazing initiative. Step by step, armed with little more than perseverance and a strong desire to help people, she managed to recruit over 1000 volunteers, launch a free crisis line, secure dedicated sponsors, raise millions of dollars and open branches throughout Australia, New Zealand, the United Kingdom and the United States. As a result of her sheer effort and dedication over the past seventeen years, Bonnie Babes has become one of the leading foundations supporting people dealing with the raw emotional pain associated with losing a child.

Bonnie Babes is not only a household name in Australia, but it also works towards reducing the number of deaths by providing lifesaving equipment to hospitals and funds for further research. Rachel Stanfield-Porter continues to be a part of the charity, passionately contributing to this cause so close to her heart.

(Bonnie Babes has recently been split into two entities: Bonnie Babes Foundation works to help vital medical research, while the Small Miracles Foundation undertakes grief counselling.)

WHAT MAKES HER AN UNDERDOG

Rachel could have been just another statistic — one in four people endures this type of loss. But she chose to turn her loss into a positive and create a place where others can now go to for support, comfort and advice.

LESSONS WE CAN LEARN FROM THIS MOTHER

- Use your loss or pain to fuel a desire to help others in similar circumstances.
- Pursue something you are passionate about and believe in.
- Feel genuinely privileged to assist others less fortunate.
- If something is broken, try to fix it.

HER TRAITS

- Sympathetic
- Relentless
- Humble
- Grateful
- Quiet achiever

HER LIGHT-BULB MOMENT

Rachel Stanfield-Porter felt compelled to help other families soon after she had lost two sons and was preparing for the birth of her fourth. She knew first-hand how hard it was to deal with the emotional pain given the lack of community support available. She decided she was going to change this and find a way to give families the much needed solace to deal with the pain they were experiencing.

Sixteen-year-old sets example for young mothers everywhere: Bernadette Black

So many people are quick to stereotype, pass judgement and dismiss the credibility and respectability of a very young mum who still looks like a child herself. It is too easy to assume these mums will not be able to finish their education and provide for their child as they have barely matured themselves. Bernadette Black challenged this view and proved that young mothers can use motherhood to become stronger women, more competent individuals and amazing role models not only for their children, but for other mothers in general, regardless of age.

Bernadette was 'a good girl' from a middle-class, church-going family who unexpectedly became pregnant at sixteen after having sex for the first time with her boyfriend of six months. She was determined to have the baby and become the best mother possible, regardless of her age, resources and how much she was being judged by family and friends. Bernadette looked for but struggled to find a supportive book or resource about other inspiring, successful young mothers.

With no one to look up to, she made the commitment to herself that, if she completed her education and become a fantastic mother, she would write the book she had needed, one full of advice, support and encouragement. She wanted to help young mothers and make them believe that they can be great, capable, educated mothers, able to provide a stable future for their children, regardless of their age.

Bernadette finished her education, became a nurse and is an amazing mother to three children who clearly adore her. She has since fulfilled her promise and written an honest, moving book, *Brave Little Bear* (the title taken from the meaning of 'Bernadette'), that gives fresh hope to thousands of other single young mothers desperate for direction, encouragement and proof that they too can turn adversity into something positive. Bernadette is also in demand as a speaker at community and school events and is the founding director of the nationwide not-for-profit charity Brave Foundation, offering ongoing support and information for people facing teenage and unplanned pregnancy. In 2009, Bernadette was awarded the national title of Barnardos Australia's Mother of the Year, and in 2008 she was a finalist for Australian of the Year for her work with young mothers and unplanned pregnancy.

WHAT MAKES HER AN UNDERDOG

- She was a sixteen-year-old child.
- She juggled high-school exams with night feeds.
- She lost her partner and many of her friends.
- She endured the judgement of society.

LESSONS WE CAN LEARN FROM THIS MOTHER

- If you have support and encouragement you can overcome your hurdles.
- Being a mother is the most important role you could ever have.
- Regardless of circumstance, you can fulfill your dreams for the future.
- Life is for living, so make sure you live it well.
- Don't be afraid to dream, live and succeed big.

HER TRAITS

- Sympathetic
- Persevering
- Loving
- Brave
- Understanding
- Hopeful

HER LIGHT-BULB MOMENT

Pregnant and determined to make life work as a young mother, Bernadette Black couldn't find a book that directly spoke to her in the way that she needed at the most traumatic time of her life. So she promised to be the person who would one day write that book, giving other young, single mothers the hope and inspiration she had needed.

Mum of nine proves anything is possible: Dr Judith Slocombe

Many of us complain how hard it is to leave the house with one, two or three children in tow, let alone to chase a personal goal. Imagine if you had nine children! Would any of us even bother to climb over the mountains of laundry, piles of dishes or toy obstacles? The thought of actually managing a tribe of eleven, a household and a successful business, while still having the time and energy to complete an MBA sounds incredibly far-fetched. Yet Dr Judith Slocombe demonstrates that the impossible is possible.

After spending ten years looking after babies and preschoolers while her career took a frustrating back seat, she set up her own veterinary pathology business, took on an MBA and figured out how to juggle children, work and personal needs so that everyone and everything was properly taken care of. In the early years of motherhood, childcare was not an economically viable option. Rather than complain that she was professionally disadvantaged, or give up her aspirations for good, she quickly learnt how to make the most of her role as part-time worker and full-time mum. She developed the skills to take her to the next part of the journey as business owner by learning to negotiate with toddlers, reason with teenagers, multi-task, delegate and prioritise.

Judith demonstrates that there are no excuses, anything is possible and motherhood should not get in the way of life or chasing your passion. You just need to continuously evaluate priorities, accommodate what is important to you, and develop the mindset to help you cope with family, work and personal needs.

WHAT MAKES HER AN UNDERDOG?

- How can anyone realistically expect to do more than manage nine children?
- Professionally, she placed her career on hold for ten years as she juggled multiple preschoolers with part-time work from home.
- Clients saw her family commitments as a negative distraction from their needs.
- She felt the need to prove herself in a male-dominated environment.

LESSONS WE CAN LEARN FROM THIS MOTHER

- Use professional setbacks as an opportunity to learn different skills that will become building blocks for your future aspirations.
- Value what you are contributing at every phase in your life.
- Address the important things now and stop worrying about the little things.
- Accept that priorities will change. Sometimes work takes precedence over family, sometimes family takes precedence over work and sometimes your needs take precedence over everything.
- Develop the mindset to have the energy to cope with everything.

- Deal with the five most important things at a time and let go of other things on your list.
- There is never a perfect time to do something you want to do, so listen to your inner voice to make the right decisions for your career, children and life.

HER TRAITS

- Determined
- Focused
- Effective
- Dedicated

HER LIGHT-BULB MOMENT

Dr Judith Slocombe was frustrated professionally while she spent a good part of a decade juggling babies and preschoolers with part-time work from home, but she soon realised that she could use the time to develop effective skills to prepare her as the owner of her own, fast-growing, award-winning business.

***

These case studies of ordinary mums who have done extraordinary things are just a few of thousands. Everywhere we look, we are surrounded by everyday mums who find the drive and desire to pursue the life they want for themselves and their families. None of them says it's an easy road. In fact, they probably all agree that it takes effort, sacrifice and determination to make it possible to do what they are doing. But by reading their stories, we can relate to their challenges and find it within ourselves to also move forward and have a go at living our dreams and being true to ourselves.

The only thing stopping you from exploring your potential is you.

Thirty traits of successful mothers

- ✓ Brave
- ✓ Committed
- ✓ Confident
- ✓ Dedicated
- ✓ Determined
- ✓ Effective
- ✓ Entrepreneurial
- ✓ Focused
- ✓ Friendly
- ✓ Generous
- ✓ Hard working
- ✓ Honest
- ✓ Humble
- ✓ Innovative
- ✓ Inspirational
- ✓ Intuitive
- ✓ Motivational
- ✓ Multi-tasker
- ✓ Optimistic
- ✓ Persistent
- ✓ Planner
- ✓ Practical
- ✓ Resilient
- ✓ Resourceful
- ✓ Responsible
- ✓ Supportive
- ✓ Tenacious
- ✓ Tough
- ✓ Visionary
- ✓ Warm

CHAPTER 24

... is for 'Visualisation techniques'

'See things as you would have them be instead of as they are. Visualise this thing that you want, see it, feel it, believe in it. Make your mental blueprint, and begin to build.'

— Robert Collier

Do you know what you want for yourself and your life? Can you clearly picture it in your mind? Or do you find yourself living with or avoiding what you don't want, without getting any closer to what you do?

More often than not, we know what we *don't* want in life. I don't want this job, this top, this house, this hairstyle, this armchair, this routine, this extra weight, this budget, this car, this, this, this … But how many of us know what we *do* want? Do you really know what your ideal job is, your ideal stay-at-home routine, your ideal body shape or what you would ideally prefer to be doing in your spare time? If you're like most of us, you'll probably find that much harder to define.

Visualisation can help you with the process of identifying what you want. It's a process of clearing your mind of the daily distractions and instead creating a mental picture of something you want to focus on achieving. It is a healthy way to establish exactly what your aspirations are and what you want to achieve in your role as both a mum and a woman.

There are countless examples of how visualisation has worked in different circumstances: from making money or recovering from an illness to beating the next set of red traffic lights! Visualisation works because the subconscious mind doesn't know the difference between something that has happened and something that is imagined to have happened, and therefore reacts in the same way. It prepares for the same outcome, whether it is a real image or a dreamed image.

If you think about what you have achieved in the past, and the thoughts and actions that led to these achievements, you will see that you visualised a lot of your decisions. You thought about how they would look before they actually materialised. You clarified your future before it happened. You are reading this because you decided you would. It was not an accident. Therefore, there is no reason, in theory, why you can't continue to decide what you want for the future as a great mum and fulfilled woman and proactively make those plans clearer.

Another well-documented use of visualisation is as an aid to giving birth. When using visualisation prior to the onset of actual labour, the aim is to create a mental image of yourself giving birth while including realistic and probable ways you could cope with the anticipated pain. You may have used this technique yourself. For example, you might see yourself in a warm bath, using a cold compress, in a dimly lit room with music on, with a supportive birth partner or with a wonderful anaesthetist. Creating the image in your mind beforehand makes the actual event more familiar and easier to handle, as you have set up your expectations, gone through a dress rehearsal, and are now better able to cope with the reality. Even if labour doesn't go exactly to plan, you will be able to draw on the positive feelings of confidence and comfort in your visualisation and adjust to the altered environment. Visualisation doesn't control unforeseen hiccups; it simply works to create a positive response.

If visualisation techniques are used for labour, there is no reason why they shouldn't be applied to other parts of a mother's daily life. Being a mother is the most 'labour'-intensive job anyway! Do you often say to yourself, 'I'm too busy being a mum to think about what I want for myself'? If so, you probably find you are stuck doing the same thing every single day, and before you know it, another week has passed by without you doing anything more extraordinary than what you did the week before. This is because the brain continues to see that you are 'too busy' and so continues the cycle of ensuring you are 'too busy'. After all, that is what you told it you are; that is the image you fed it. You need to change the image to change the outcome.

Visualisation techniques can come in handy during other trying times of motherhood. There are days where breastfeeding issues can really depress you, fluctuating hormones send you all over the place and an unsettled baby can shatter your self-confidence. You may hate your routine or feel personally and professionally out of place because you are no longer working in the environment you have been used to for so many years. These are all common experiences of women entering motherhood. These experiences can all challenge our mindset, belief in ourselves and our ability to move forward into a happy, fulfilled and productive future.

So while visualisation might sound clichéd, it can effectively boost your self-esteem and attitude so that you feel you really can handle motherhood and overcome any hurdles on your way to achieving your personal needs and aspirations. Similar to hypnosis, visualisation works as a powerful mind suggestion — if you really want it to work. If you continue to have negative thoughts and feelings, you will have a negative reaction. So each time you think negative, replace that thought with a positive image or affirmation.

When you are ready to focus on what you want, be prepared to put in some time initially to clearly pinpoint what that actually is. It does take time and mental effort to get the vision in place, but once you have it established, all you need to do is keep on revisiting it as a reminder and continue to take the necessary steps to making it a reality. When life becomes manic, at least you have a clear vision to go back to.

The benefits of visualisation

It's relaxing and relieves stress

- It's a chance to quiet the mind and think something pleasant.
- It's an escape from the daily grind.
- It's like yoga for the mind.

You feel happy

- It can be quite uplifting and joyous as it feels like you are already living it.
- Your brain responds in the same way it would if it really did happen.
- Visualising it is the next best thing to actually having it!

A means of creative expression

- You get to be creative and literally watch yourself 'think big'.
- It takes you away from your comfort zone.
- You enter a world where you can do anything and be anyone.

Refocusing tool

- Visualisation helps you clear the clutter from your mind.
- By doing this you refocus on your core aspirations and connect with your goals.
- You have a clearer objective and know where you are heading.

Confidence boost

- You are more confident because you feel like it has nearly happened anyway.
- The more you keep visualising, the more you believe in the possibilities.
- Confidence makes you more likely to take steps to realising goals in real life.

Me time

- It feels indulgent as it's time for you to think about yourself.
- It's invigorating having no limits, no boundaries and no rules for what you can do and achieve.
- You explore your inner voice and get to 'see' what the 'what ifs' in your mind look like.

And best of all, it's free!

Here is a basic four-step process to implementing visualisation techniques, regardless of how crazy your daily life is. Whether you want to overcome the pain barrier when breastfeeding, feel good about your body again, kick start a brand new career or enjoy your new lifestyle as a stay-at-home mum, these steps will see you through. Of course, you are not going to win the lottery without buying a ticket or lose weight without a healthy diet and exercise, so some effort is required. The trick is to decide what you want first, and then it is easier to fill in the gaps regarding how you go about getting there.

STEP 1: FIND SOME QUIET TIME

For example:

- Before the kids wake up.
- Before you go to bed.
- In the shower.
- In the bath.
- While walking with the pram.

STEP 2: PICK SOMETHING TO FOCUS ON

For example:

- What your dream job is.
- What your ideal body shape is.
- Where your next holiday destination should be.
- What breastfeeding effortlessly looks like.
- What your ideal routine is.

STEP 3: CREATE YOUR IDEAL MENTAL BLUEPRINT

For example:

- Use all your senses to picture the scene clearly.
- Ask yourself some questions to bring the scene to life, such as:
    - How does it make you feel?
    - What details can you see?
    - What are you saying in the image?
- You can also write down your goals and/or create a vision board.

STEP 4: REPEAT

- Continue to visit the image, list or vision board as often as you can, especially during your quiet time.
- Remember, we become what we think about the most.

If you are normally a pragmatic person, or perhaps even a 'glass half empty' type, it is easy to baulk at the idea of visualisation and all the spiritual connotations it normally comes with. In this instance, let's put aside all the heavy breathing and Zen-like state and concentrate more on the practical side of visualisation. All we are doing is clearing our minds of the day-to-day clutter so that we can really focus on the core things we want for ourselves. When we have stripped back our thoughts to the basic message or goal we want to achieve, it is so much easier to hold on to that image, chase that image and achieve that image.

As a mum, you probably have a million thoughts going on in your mind and just as many things on the go. So to finally clear your head and decide where you want to go with your life takes a big effort, but it's well worth it. After all, you can't move forward if you don't know where you're going.

CHAPTER 25

W

... is for
'Working and the Wonder Woman myth'

'Just because I choose to do something that I love, that doesn't make me a worse mum.'

— Trina (40), mum to Benjamin (ten) and Andrew (seven)

At some point, most women will be faced with a decision: do they return to work, stay at home to be the primary homemaker, or do a little bit of both? While we all want to do our best for our children and give them the best life possible, there is no easy answer as to which is the right choice.

All mothers should be admired and respected for the difficult decisions they make. Stay-at-home mums make their own sacrifices to be home. Working mums face difficulties as they deal with the guilt of not being present with their children full time. But both have a common goal: to be the best mum possible. There is no point judging yourself or others for choosing to work or not, as we all have our own personal reasons for doing what we know is best for us and our families.

Not everyone has the choice to be a stay-at-home mum. Many families have large mortgages and an increasing cost of living to accommodate, and just don't have the support and resources available to raise a family without two incomes. Other mums choose to work because they have spent countless hours getting degrees and building impressive careers and genuinely love their contribution outside the home. Work brings out their best and many miss the extra source of stimulation when they're at home with baby.

If you have made the decision to go back to work, expect some changes. You will now be juggling two jobs — that of employee and that of mum. Be prepared for the guilt. You will feel guilty for leaving your child in care, you will feel guilty for missing milestones, you will feel guilty for not being able to work late nights, and you will feel guilty that you sometimes have to say 'no' to your employer, your child, family and friends. Some days will be better than others and there are things you can do to appease the guilt.

For example, make sure you trust, respect and share the same values as the person caring for your child. If you know that your child is in brilliant hands, enjoying educational, fun experiences, there is no need to feel bad. You can speak with your employer about taking some work home, so that if you feel you have left the office in a rush, you can complete tasks when the baby has gone to bed. And when you do feel on top of your game, take on an extra work project or reconnect with family you have neglected. That way you make up for the times you had to say 'no'.

You might also need to rethink your career ambitions. You might still be as hungry as ever for the next step up in your career, but it might be downright impossible to strive for that next step if it means constant travel or hours you can't commit to. However, this doesn't mean you can never progress professionally. It simply means you have to think outside the square. Perhaps the same role in a different company closer to home would be more beneficial. Perhaps you could work from home some of the time, or job share. Continue to focus on the career you want but think about alternative ways in which it can fit into your life.

'When I went back to work, I started working even harder and smarter than I did before I had a child. I wanted to prove that, just because I was a mum, that didn't mean I wouldn't be up for any new challenges. I was working hard, but still left at 5 p.m. every day to pick up my baby from childcare. I proved that, as a mum, I was an even better employee because I could multi-task, prioritise, delegate and think outside the square. I worked part time, ran out the door at 5 p.m. on the days I was in and demanded my pay rise every time. I deserved it.'

— Janine (30), mum to Allira (two)

You might have good intentions to work, but have difficulties dedicating the same time and energy that you used to. You might have to leave at 5 p.m. sharp to pick up baby, or can't attend breakfast meetings or presentations because it is impossible to drop off a child at 6 a.m. at childcare. You might not have the home support available to attend conferences or working weekends.

This is frustrating for mums. As much as you want to be at work, performing professionally, you have to accept you will encounter some restrictions. To overcome them, you can discuss different strategies with your employer. For example, you might not be able to physically attend breakfast meetings, but you can via a conference call. Or you can attend working bees for part of the weekend. Fortunately, there are an increasing number of companies providing family-friendly work practices that recognise and accommodate real-life restrictions.

'My manager told me, "We didn't invite you to the breakfast presentation because we figured it would have been too hard for you to attend with the kids to organise." I was taken aback by this because, as far as I was concerned, I made a commitment to work for them. It should have been my call if I could make it or not. I just felt like they disregarded my value now that I have extra family commitments.'

— Sam (34), mum to Bradley (four) and Grace (one)

Full-time, 9 a.m.–5 p.m. work is not the only option for mums who want or need to go back to work. There is casual work, part-time work, shift work and contract work. People can work from home, job share or freelance. And there's also self-employment to consider. There are many helpful employment resources that actually target mothers wanting to return to work and provide greater information on the different work options available and how they can better suit your new lifestyle.

As challenging as it is to fit in another job when you are already doing the most important job of all, there are actually many benefits to being a working mother. Working provides an opportunity to get time alone away from the day-to-day madness. You also have the chance to interact with adults and develop your identity beyond that of being a mum. Plus you get paid for what you do! It's also setting a positive, realistic example for your children, who will also have to go to work one day.

Two added benefits of working are that you get to go to the toilet without an audience and can finish a coffee before it gets cold! Only a mum understands how rare this is. When you are at home it is impossible to get some peace and quiet, especially if you are taking care of babies and toddlers. Working will give you that temporary quiet time and the opportunity to focus on something other than your children's relentless demands for your time and attention. You even get a lunch break — imagine that, a lunch break!

'I knew it was time to go back to work when I was out for dinner with my husband at a beautiful restaurant and I turned and said to him, "Mummy give you some water?" That wasn't the only incident. Earlier that week I walked into a café and saw some old colleagues. I don't know what came over me, but instead of saying something normal like, "Hi, how are you going?", I actually said to them, "Aaah boo!" They just stared at me and I felt like an utter d#@khead. I had truly forgotten how to talk to adults.'

— Monica (33), mum to Olivia and Rosie (three)

As our children get older and start incessantly sharing their thoughts, feelings and funny stories, it can be a lot of fun spending time with them just listening to what they say and how they view the world around them. They can be so entertaining. But every now and again, you need to get out of that bubble and chat to others closer to your age. It is healthy for us as adults to continue to be able to relate to one another, away from the park and play centres.

A working environment will give you the chance to reconnect with different personalities and people with varied backgrounds, and converse with them about life, events, business and pleasure. Of course, stay-at-home mums also interact with adults, but a work environment can provide the opportunity to liaise with a more diverse set of people, more regularly.

A common topic of discussion among mothers who have just started maternity leave is the fact that you feel like you have lost your identity now that you are no longer working. You might have been an accountant, a marketing manager, a graphic artist, a sales coordinator, a lawyer, a receptionist, etc. Your job shaped who you were. Now, you spend most of your time washing, feeding, bathing, cooking, shopping, singing nursery rhymes and going to the park.

Even though being a great mum is your priority, you no longer experience that sense of pride, achievement and satisfaction from using your mind to finish a demanding project, negotiate a deal or bring in new business. Going back to work can re-introduce some of those feelings and make you feel like you are still that balanced, talented woman who can accomplish many things.

We need money to live, to provide for our families and to secure our future. There is nothing wrong with playing an active part in physically contributing to the finances. Sure, the trade-off is that we physically don't spend as much time with our children, but by working we can provide stability, family essentials and the freedom to do and buy more of the things we were accustomed to having before children. More money coming into the household can mean family life is not burdened with financial woes.

Some families can afford to have a parent at home full time; others don't value materialistic extras. But if this is not you, you shouldn't feel greedy or selfish because you are working to pay for a future that you believe is important for you and your family. Our children will grow up and have to work. It is healthy for children to understand, even from a young age, that although family is a key priority, working can also be mentally and personally rewarding. They learn that to have the toys, gadgets and karate lessons, someone has to work for it and work can actually be fun. Working is another way to demonstrate financial values and also show how mums are on an equal footing with dads.

By working and leaving our children in the care of others, we are also preparing our children for pre-school environments, where different people are responsible for them. This can be great for their independence as they learn other ways of doing things and relating to people. Children can also relish a greater freedom to challenge themselves, without overprotective mum screaming, 'No!' in the distance. They also learn how to cope and feel secure when mum and dad are not present.

How you can get back into the workforce after a period of absence

- Put together a résumé. Familiarise yourself with the latest ways to write and present it. Then get someone else to review it — ideally someone familiar with the industry you are interested in.

- Include any volunteer work you are involved in, groups you are a part of and different skills you have picked up since you last had a paying job.

- Look for jobs in the paper, online and on notice boards. Contact ex-employers and tell friends and anyone you chat with that you are in the market for a job.

- Discuss your passions or any hobby in which you invest a lot of time and effort. You will definitely be able to find some transferable skills to include on your résumé.

- Look at what you can do to start your own business and contact your local government and council to find out what free support, resources and networks are available to help you get started.

- Research any company that would like to interview you so that you are well informed and can ask relevant questions. This will help you maintain a professional discussion about the organisation and how you are suited to it.

- Dress appropriately and professionally for interviews to demonstrate you are serious. As a rule of thumb, dress slightly above their standard dress code.

- Know your strengths and practise interview questions. Be prepared to prove how you are an asset.

- Sign up to relevant job boards and meet with several recruitment companies. Keep in contact with recruiters regularly so that you are at the top of their list when a suitable job does come up.

- Be determined but realistic about your job expectations and capabilities.
- If you know you will eventually go back to work, during your time of absence make an effort to keep in touch with colleagues and key contacts who could assist you in the future.
- Where possible, keep your qualifications current. You might need to complete a short course or some job training before you return to work.
- Understand that finding a job does take time. Don't be disheartened by rejections. Every 'no' brings you one step closer to a 'yes'. Learn from each interview so that you are aware of what to do better next time.

How you can better juggle work and family commitments

Your work, life and family balance will never be picture perfect all the time. That's just reality. There will always be turbulence, unexpected incidents and times when you are doing more of this or more of that at the expense of something else. The important thing is that you continue to monitor and *move towards* having more balance before something (or someone) falls apart. If you maintain some control over the whole juggling act, you will feel more confident that the important people (including yourself), projects and obligations are getting the attention they deserve.

There are many different things you can do to promote work–life balance, including:

1. Cook meals in bulk and freeze them so that you don't always have to race home from work and spend 45 minutes cooking.
2. Spend real, quality time with your child away from the chores, TV,

BlackBerry or iPhone. This way you know you are an active, present parent when you are around, so that you don't need to feel guilty when you are not.

3. If you can afford help such as a cleaner or ironing person, this will free up more family time.

4. Before you start work, discuss with your partner how you are each going to assist with other obligations and family commitments, such as pick-ups, drop-offs, cooking and cleaning. It's helpful to know in advance how and if you can manage.

5. Don't try to be perfect at everything. It is not realistic to have a perfectly clean household all the time, be working, get eight hours sleep a night and spend two hours a day of quality time with your child and partner. Spend your time and energy on things that matter and reconsider the other things that don't.

6. Depending on your resources and how well you are coping as a family with you working, it might pay to review work options. It might be better if you reduced your hours and only worked part time instead of full time. Or if you did contract work or worked from home, so you didn't spend hours commuting.

7. Combine tasks. You can go for a walk with your partner and the baby to the park. This way you exercise, spend quality time talking with your partner and entertain the baby.

8. Pack lunches and lay out clothes the night before.

9. Ask for and accept help when others are willing to assist you with babysitting, cooking and cleaning. This way you gain some time to slow down, do something for you, spend time with your partner and just relax as a family.

10. Keep your sense of humour. It's the only thing that will get you through

some really trying moments, like when you have to explain to your manager that you were late for work because your toddler kept taking his clothes off and it took you twenty minutes to strap him in his seat because he was having a tantrum.

11. Take care of yourself so that you don't burn out. Recognise the signs and take a breather when you know it is all getting too much.

12. Say 'no' when you have to.

The Wonder Woman myth

Ever since the feminist movement, women have continually been told that they can have it all. We can have the career, the relationship and the family. Yet it is only when we finally get the degree, climb the corporate ladder, meet Prince Charming and pop out a baby that we realise that having it all, doing it all and being everything to everyone comes at a price.

It is difficult to keep all the wheels spinning given the pressure and pace of modern life. We learn that being a wonder woman or supermum requires too much blood, sweat, tears and sacrifice. Even if we can juggle 50 hats, is it worth it? Or are we left too busy, stressed, preoccupied and overscheduled to appreciate the journey? When we

stretch past our tipping point and subsequently fall to pieces, we feel like failures because we expected to succeed in everything we set out to do. That's when it's time to review what *honestly* makes us happy, not perfect.

Women are not 'settling' if they just chase what matters to them and let go of the rest. It is healthier in the long run to be living a life that truly reflects your beliefs and fundamental priorities, rather than trying to live a hugely chaotic life dictated by society's perceived standards. Perhaps you need to walk away from a high-pressure job, live in a smaller home to afford a family, or take on part-time work to fund growing expenses. You are not failing; you are recognising that priorities have shifted.

At some stage in life, your priority will be to get pregnant and raise a child. At another point, it will be to re-enter the workforce, and at yet another point it will be to set yourself up financially. We can't always have everything — baby, money and career — at the same time. Something has to give so that you can properly care for your family and yourself as you move through the stages in life.

The following quote I heard captured in a nutshell the Wonder Woman myth and the quest to 'have it all':

'If you are breathing, walking and have your five senses you have it all. Everything else is secondary. Life is what you make of it so let's stop the whining and worrying and make the best of what we have.'

— Unknown

CHAPTER 26

... is for 'X-factor'

Can you remember meeting seemingly ordinary people in your life who were totally magnetic, interesting and just 'had something about them'? They might not have been overly attractive, funny or fashionable and sometimes they probably weren't even nice or likeable. Yet these people all had something in common. Whether you liked them or hated them, you remembered them and were drawn to some element of their presence you couldn't quite identify. They just had 'it'. By 'it' I mean that certain something you can't put your finger on but which makes them all the more intriguing.

It is called the X-factor.

The X-factor is what separates something or someone ordinary from the extraordinary. It is the 'thing' that draws others' full attention. It's not looks. It's not wardrobe. It's not entirely attitude. It is an element of your attractiveness as a person that comes from the inside and makes its way out.

Some people would argue that you either have the X-factor or you don't — you can't pretend to have it. It's an intrinsic quality, not something that can be mistaken for great perfume or pretty clothes. The X-factor is a combination of your energy, attitude and what you do with what you've got.

Think back to a moment in your past when you really felt like you had 'it'. Maybe you used to get every job you applied for, could make a room full of businesspeople stop and listen, or could walk into any VIP event without an invitation or have sales assistants keen to serve you first. You just had a glow about you that drew people in. Men, women and opportunities were always attracted to you.

You knew it had little to do with your looks, your clothes or your credentials. It came from somewhere within you and others just simply picked up on it. Even they were probably puzzled by what was so special about you. Whatever it was, you had it.

That is, until you entered motherhood.

'What has happened to me? I used to go to bars and be picked out of the queue for priority access. My restaurant tabs were quietly paid for by secret admirers. Clients were a blubbering mess around me. I could work an outfit from a discount store.

I'm not even the smartest, prettiest, coolest or funniest. Never have been, but I could stop traffic and demand attention. I was average, inside and out, but I knew I had a glow and a charisma that opened doors.

Now, I just blend in, barely. I am so ordinary, even I forget myself. The only thing I seem to attract now is the creepy-looking guy from the gym. What happened to my mojo? I want my X-factor back.'

— Melissa (32), mum to Valerie (two)

Have you seen *your* X-factor lately, or is it hidden underneath a pile of washing with your name on it? A change of routine, demands, wardrobe, body shape and lifestyle can naturally make you feel a little more ordinary these days. After all, you are spending more time in a sandpit than attending hot new bar openings, you're wearing sneakers rather than Chanel, and you have one-way conversations with toothless dribblers who don't even know what you're talking about. Realistically, you don't need your X-factor to get through your day; you need reliable breast pads. You can spend the day with vomit on your top and un-brushed teeth and you can still get your job done.

Just because you don't need to reclaim your X-Factor to be a mum and do what you are doing, that doesn't mean you should get used to being a little less fabulous. You're not always going to be wiping bottoms and soaking stains. You will re-enter the world. You will reclaim a social life and hang out with friends again. You will have other opportunities in life that will take you on to the next part of your journey. So you have every reason to hold on to your personal spark.

'I saw my ex recently at a café and he looked pretty good. I, on the other hand, ran the other way and crossed my fingers he didn't recognise me. I was having a particularly bad moment. Baby had pooped all the way up to her neck (honestly, how do they do that?), my toddler was having a bit of a meltdown because she dropped her ice-cream, and I was wearing the clothes I'd slept in the night before. (Not technically pyjamas, not technically a tracksuit — they were somewhere in between, which is probably worse.)

Needless to say, I looked like a mess and hardly projected the "look-what-you-missed-out-on" look. The last time we saw each other I was on top of the world. I had just got back from an overseas holiday and was about to start my dream job. I was confident, sassy and vibrant. It made me think that's how I always want to be described.

I didn't want to be described as "tired, stressed and boring". It was a wake-up call to remind me that, even though I was a mum, and part of that role includes changing nappies and negotiating with a three-year-old, I still deserve to look and feel amazing and more like the person I remember. I don't actually want to look and feel like someone who just changes nappies and cowers to a child all day.'

— Whitney (36), mum to Stanley (three) and Radha (one)

It can be a little unsettling for mums to look in the mirror and know that a part of their glow has disappeared. At this point in our lives we are doing so much more for other people's wellbeing. The pressure and full-time responsibility does take its toll and something has to give.

We are forced to sacrifice something of ours — such as our time, energy and resources — so that others around us can have it all. We give up our careers, part of our identity, our social lives, looks, beauty appointments, and so much more. In the beginning we might appear okay on the outside, but don't be fooled. On the inside we can start to fall apart as a result of giving up too much of ourselves.

When we neglect ourselves a bit too much, a small but key part of us withers away, and it shows on the outside. You are left feeling and looking rather ordinary and depleted, when you really want to look and feel alive, vibrant, attractive, valued, healthy, interesting and interested. You want to shine in life, as a person, mother and woman.

For those of us who left our X-factor somewhere on the birthing suite floor or who are totally baffled by the concept and wonder if they even had it in the first place, there are still things you can do to capture that magic. There is no secret formula to getting 'it', but here are some suggestions that have worked for other mums. These suggestions have given mothers a more positive energy and attitude, and a renewed confidence, inside and out.

How to re-ignite your X-factor

- Smile more often.
- Work your best asset.
- Make an effort with your looks.
- Have a positive attitude.
- Feel confident in your appearance.
- Freshen up your look with a new hair- or make-up style.
- Be polite to others.
- Do something selfless for someone else.
- Be a good listener.
- Boost your self-esteem.
- Reconnect with friends you love.
- Laugh more often.
- Spend some time on your own.
- Flirt with your partner again.
- Strengthen your strengths.
- Learn something new.
- Surround yourself with people who inspire you.
- Find hobbies you enjoy.
- Shake up your routine.
- Push yourself out of your comfort zone.
- Find a job you love.
- Let go of the past and anything that is holding you back.
- Stop whinging.
- Do something different, more often.

- Have a rest and nurture your mind and body.
- Remind yourself of your accomplishments.
- Be true to yourself and what you want, not what others expect.
- Get a mentor, life coach or someone to guide you.
- Reflect on parts of your life when you really felt alive to remind yourself what you are looking for and what you are capable of feeling.
- Expect the best.

While you pay attention to what's going on around you in life, give the same amount of attention to what is happening to you on the inside. Life and circumstances have changed, but as you settle into your routine, do what you have to do to keep that spark in yourself alive, even if it is trickier at times to do so.

You deserve to be true to yourself and feel good about who you are, where you are going and how you are living. When you reconnect and accommodate your values, needs and dreams you will feel more like the person you remember. Then you can honestly project that X-factor to the world. You will have a positive energy, the right attitude and be making the most of what you've got, inside and out.

CHAPTER 27

Y

... is for 'You and your needs'

Now that you're a mother, it doesn't take long to fully recognise and appreciate the significance of your new role. It is incredibly daunting, wonderful and horrible, all at the same time, to be a woman with the weighty responsibility of grooming a little human for life in the big, scary world! So you need to be fit: mentally, physically and emotionally. And to address your mental, physical and emotional wellness, you need to do more for *your* life and you as an individual, not just as a mother. This chapter is all about why you need to take care of yourself for the long haul. It will help you to recognise the causes and symptoms of self-neglect while showing you easy ways to accommodate and prioritise your personal needs, desires and dreams as a woman.

'Just the thought of doing something for myself, buying something for myself or even wanting to be by myself makes me feel guilty. I feel like I shouldn't and that I always need to be doing something for others, buying stuff for the kids instead of me and that I need to be with the kids the whole time, otherwise I wonder, "Am I really a good mum?"

But then, on the other hand, sometimes I am scared of what will happen to me if I don't just run away from it all every now and again. I love my family, but the constant demands drive me crazy and when I reach my tipping point I must get away just to recharge and relax.

Motherhood is relentless. A constant cycle and someone always wants a piece of me. It just won't stop. That's why sometimes I need to put my hand up and say, "I need a break." I need to take care of myself too, otherwise I *will* fall apart, either physically, emotionally or both.'

— Galit (36), mum to Jay (seven), Derek (five) and Abdiel (one)

If you don't prioritise your needs as a woman and take care of your mind, body and attitude, you can slowly fall apart without even realising it's happening. It is actually easier to neglect your needs than it is to care for them. The additional pressures that come with motherhood can consume you and make it absolutely impossible for you to do anything other than take care of your child. And sometimes, even that is too hard a task. That is, unless you know what to do to address your personal requirements, away from motherhood, without sacrificing the needs of your loved ones.

Things that lead to self-neglect

- A fear that you are not doing enough for your child, so you keep trying to do more.
- Lack of sleep.

- Increased demands in your life meaning there is less time for what you were used to doing.
- The pressure you place on yourself to keep up with what the books/parents/other mums tell you to do.
- An unrealistic expectation that you can be on call 24 hours a day and still perform at optimum levels at all times.
- Not enough time to rest and recharge, so you're left feeling depleted.
- Trying to still be the perfect wife, daughter, friend, carer, all while juggling a newborn's demands.
- Not having enough outside help, which makes it difficult to complete even the most basic task.
- A lack of supportive relationships or people close to you to guide you and encourage you to take care of your needs.

Recognising the symptoms of self-neglect is as simple as stopping what you are doing and listening to your inner voice. What is your body trying to tell you? Give yourself a basic mental, emotional and physical health check. Are you happy? Sad? Lonely? Bored? Desperate? Hungry? Tired? Stressed? Unhealthy? Neglected? Is everything under control and are you still in control? Don't lie to yourself.

It is important to recognise the symptoms of self-neglect and take action so that you continue to thrive as an individual. You deserve to be the star in your journey and your life overall, not just as a mum, so you can properly lead the way for your children. This sounds easy enough to do, but when you only have about five spare minutes a day, it can be hard to find time to go to the bathroom, never mind pay attention to your 'inner voice' and what you think you need. Luckily, however, it doesn't take long to figure out what you need to do to function better, not only as a parent, but also, importantly, as a woman.

Symptoms of self-neglect

- No longer doing anything for yourself the way you used to; i.e. exercise, beauty routine, regular massages, shopping, work, socialising.
- Loss of interest in yourself.
- Depression and anxiety.
- Exhaustion.
- Finding it hard to sleep.
- Lack of interest in normally pleasurable activities.
- No sex drive.
- Increased reliance on drugs or alcohol.
- Headaches and muscle tension.
- Stomach complaints.
- Getting sick more often.
- Change in appetite.
- Trouble concentrating.
- Negative outlook.
- Sense of failure.
- Withdrawal from society and social engagements.
- Boredom most of the day.
- Feeling underappreciated.
- Feeling overwhelmed.
- Lack of confidence in making simple decisions.
- Lashing out at others.
- Having more 'bad' days than 'good' days.
- Sense of failure.
- Lack of motivation.
- Low self-esteem.
- Feeling alone or detached from life.
- No sense of accomplishment.

If you do take the time to address your needs, you will have a healthy mind, body and attitude. These will make you better equipped to successfully and happily handle life as a woman who is also a mother. There is a catch, though. To achieve this, you need to be responsible for yourself. No one will feed you the right foods, whisper affirmations in your ear or cheer you on when you've done a good job. You need to take control and take action for yourself.

It only takes some very basic changes to make a difference. So, you can still take charge of your needs even when you are consumed with your newborn's demands. The trick is to make small changes often and then be consistent. That way the gradual changes you are making are easier for you to adopt as well as being easier for everyone else to accept. These small changes might seem insignificant at first but collectively they will shape a much brighter routine and stay with you for life.

There is no point taking a week off motherhood to go to a spa retreat if you come back to exactly the same routine and stress levels. Just as there is no point joining a gym and visiting it five times a week for the first three weeks but then never again. Or swearing off alcohol only to binge drink a month later.

If you want to start exercising, commit to a realistic number of times per week — that might only be twice a week. If you want your husband to help with cooking, agree that every Tuesday night he cooks. If you want to eat more healthily, swap your daily chocolate bar habit for a low-fat chocolate biscuit. Just keep on making small changes, often, and be consistent.

Small steps that can bring big changes for you

- Slow down.
- Make exercise part of your routine.
- Address and treat any physical ailments.

- Improve your eating habits.
- Drink less alcohol.
- Learn to manage stress.
- Get more sleep.
- Reduce commitments.
- Set some boundaries and learn to say 'no'.
- Re-evaluate your priorities.
- Create a more balanced schedule that includes family time, me time and couple time.
- Get up fifteen minutes earlier to get something done for yourself.
- Get more organised.
- Spend money on yourself.
- Spend time away from your normal environment.
- Plan your day or schedule so that you stop chasing your tail.
- Stop and have a break every day.
- Talk to someone or join a support group.
- Don't try to be perfect at everything.
- Share babysitting duties with a friend so you can schedule more personal time.
- Be more positive.
- Adopt a relaxing ritual.
- Do something just for you.
- Make an effort to see your friends.
- Enjoy what you do.
- Pamper yourself.
- Rediscover what really makes you happy.

You can only give the best of yourself when you have the best of yourself to offer. It is not selfish to prioritise your needs and put yourself first. Taking care of you is a responsible way to prevent personal breakdowns, burnout and a hopeless outlook. By doing so, you are caring for yourself and making sure you are properly geared up for the challenge of taking care of baby. And you will do an even better job as a result. You will be rested, energised, healthy, happy and able to be a strong, competent, reliable, patient, balanced and secure role model for your child. The better *you* feel, the better equipped you will be to handle the demanding days, sleepless nights and all the unknowns in between.

CHAPTER 28

... is for more 'Zing when you're zonked!'

It is no surprise that some people (most definitely new parents) view sleep deprivation as a form of torture. It is impossible to function far less survive for too long without some decent shut-eye. Lack of sleep is one thing, but when combined with a sore body, wild hormones and a lack of experience, sleep deprivation takes on a whole new meaning. It is, however, something we can learn to deal with.

Of course you are overcome by exhaustion. You have just spent 40 weeks carrying a little life inside you. This was then followed by twenty hours in labour and five days entertaining 50 million visitors. You've probably had a total of four minutes' uninterrupted sleep since you gave birth. Then, battered, bruised and overwhelmed, you are sent packing from hospital. It's time to go home and face it all on your own.

You feel like you've been hit by a bus. All you want is to lie down in bed for a few days to rest and recover. All you need is some peace and quiet. If you could just have a few days to yourself to get over the pregnancy and labour, you know that you'd be okay. That's not too much to ask, is it? Just a few days to catch up on lost sleep?

But those days never come. You are expected to perform immediately. You need to feed. You need to burp. Settle. Soothe. Every two hours. Then you need to do it again and again and again. Sometimes for weeks before you get any respite. There is simply no time for you to sleep. The demands are relentless.

Before you gave birth, everybody rambled on about how you should catch up on your sleep before the baby was born. They warned you there would be sleepless nights. And you knew, of course, that your slumber would suffer some interruptions. But seriously, the reality is just so extreme! You could never have predicted how bad you would feel.

'In the first five weeks, sleep deprivation left me a groggy mess. All I could think about was my next hit of caffeine. I would crack open an energy drink … to keep me going while I waited for my coffee to boil … to drink before I picked up a real coffee from the café down the road. All my friends kept reassuring me that things would get better. I was not convinced.

But they were right. Baby and I are managing to sleep a little more these days and I stand before you as a recovering caffeine addict.'

— Paige (29), mum to Antoinette (six months)

In the early weeks and sometimes months, it is impossible to carry on doing everything you used to do before sleep was interrupted. There really is no need to be a supermum. You can't cook, clean, shop, socialise and keep other children entertained as you did before if you don't get enough sleep. The exhaustion will overcome you and your body will just crash until it is replenished.

Sleep is vital to your wellbeing. A lack of it can leave you feeling emotional, vulnerable, irritable, stressed, anxious, depressed and disoriented. Without sleep, your body struggles to mentally and physically repair itself. As a result of sleep deprivation, you are left so fatigued, both mentally and physically, that some days even the simplest tasks or decisions are beyond you.

'Some days I was so tired I couldn't recall if I fed the baby during the night or even how or if I managed to put the baby back to bed. I was so sleep deprived I was borderline delirious.'

— Adelaide (36), mum to Seth (four)

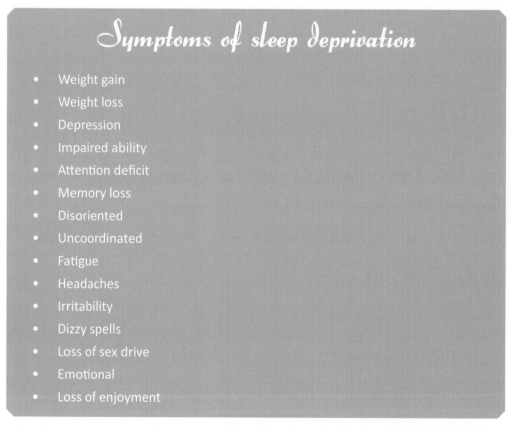

Symptoms of sleep deprivation

- Weight gain
- Weight loss
- Depression
- Impaired ability
- Attention deficit
- Memory loss
- Disoriented
- Uncoordinated
- Fatigue
- Headaches
- Irritability
- Dizzy spells
- Loss of sex drive
- Emotional
- Loss of enjoyment

For the first four or five months, it is not uncommon to lose around two hours' sleep a night. Then after this time, you may only lose one hour a night. But in those first three months, when the sleep deprivation is at its worst, how are you supposed to live? What do you do if your child continues to wake throughout the night long after the books say they should? You can't just exit from life until you feel rested, can you?

There are many experienced mothers out there who know that it is actually possible to function and cope reasonably well even if you don't get your normal eight hours of shut-eye. You might not initially be doing as much as you were before baby, but it is amazing what our mind and bodies can do and what we are capable of enduring. Mother Nature has a funny way of preparing us for life as a parent to a teenage driver, when sleep deprivation again rears its ugly head!

Some mums cope by catching up on sleep during the day, while other mums find they get more sleep if the baby (safely) co-sleeps with them. You might not even need extra sleep, and find lying down in the bath or reading a magazine is sufficient. Everyone is different, but the objective is the same and that is to replenish the mind and body.

How we can get more sleep

- Sleep when baby sleeps.
- Co-sleep (safely) with baby.
- Accept offers of help.
- Enlist grandparents to help with babysitting.
- Get to bed earlier.
- Express milk so a partner can assist during night feeds.
- Get baby into a more predictable sleep routine.
- Let go of the domestic front to gain more sleep time.
- Hire a night nurse.

Some nights you have the best intentions of catching up on sleep by going to bed early, but just can't fall asleep. Or there may be nights when your baby takes longer to feed and resettle. Then when you do finally get baby back to sleep you find yourself wide awake. If you struggle to fall asleep in the first place, or to get back to sleep after a night feed, there are some natural remedies that can assist.

How we can get to sleep more easily

- Reduce caffeine intake during the day.
- Spend time winding down before going to bed.
- Don't think about how hard it is to fall asleep.
- Spray your pillow with lavender.
- Drink some warm milk or relaxing herbal tea.
- Listen to relaxing music.
- Have a warm bath.
- Get your partner to give you a massage.
- Try sleeping in a different room.
- Invest in heavy curtains or blackout blinds.

As unbelievable as it sounds, you only have to cope with severe lack of sleep for the first few months. It is not going to be like this forever. Even at three months you will find that babies can sleep for six-hour stretches, if not longer, and your body will have a chance to catch up on lost sleep. In the meantime, you can lift your energy levels by eating the right foods, lying down, going for a walk and cutting back on non-essential items on your 'to do' list.

How to feel re-energised (without sleeping)

- Go for a walk.
- Lie down.
- Shower.
- Get a massage.
- Do less housework.
- Burn essential oils.
- Eat nutritious, low GI foods.
- Learn to meditate.
- Stay hydrated.
- Get out of your sleepwear.

You will have your good days and you will have your bad days, or bad weeks, that seem to go on forever and make it difficult to catch up on rest. You will be left so exhausted that no amount of caffeine can help you. And then you will find yourself emotional, breaking down and crying over little things. Ongoing lack of sleep leaves you feeling more sensitive and believing that everything is much worse than it really is.

When you feel like this, focus on getting through the day and trust that with each day that passes it will get easier. But before you reach your tipping point, ask for some help and don't overload yourself with too many demands. If sleep does not improve and you cannot cope or are starting to feel angry and resentful, chat to your doctor or healthcare professional. Sometimes just talking to your partner or other mums about how you are feeling can help. You might find that some comfort, reassurance and a hug is all you need to soldier on.

On the bright side, sleep deprivation is a rite of passage for a new parent: the welcome gift! It is also temporary and you will get through this foggy period. But don't be surprised if you do put milk in the oven, fall asleep at the dinner table and wear mismatched shoes in the meantime.

'I have just woken up from a three-month slumber. I didn't realise how tired I was until now. The world around me looks different now. I can string a sentence together, I can remember where I put things, I can bring myself to socialise and I can even plan for tomorrow. Amazing what sleep can do! Bring out the violins, even the grass looks greener.'

— Caitlyn (34), mum to Ebony (three) and Iris (three months)

TEN THINGS THEY DON'T TELL YOU

Misconceptions about motherhood

1. We can have it all, but not at the same time and hardly in equal doses. Something always has to give.

2. You won't know who you are anymore after you have a baby and it takes time, effort and heartache to get to know and develop this new you.

3. Motherhood can actually be boring at times. You will fantasise about being somewhere else doing something different.

4. Some days you will cry, behave and sound like an absolute nutcase. The next day, you will be perfectly fine, like nothing happened. Raging hormones, isolation, new demands and uncertainty will do that to you occasionally.

5. You will never have peace of mind again. You're always scared something will happen to your child, you or your partner that will get in the way of giving your baby the perfect, blessed, healthy life they deserve.

6. It becomes a lot harder to chase your dreams, aspirations and desires now that you are a mum. It takes much more effort, motivation and dedication to do something for you than it does to just get on with chores, homework, flash cards and going to the park.

7. Sex can be better, raunchier and more enjoyable than ever before.

8. You lose control of your life. As much as you plan and expect baby to fit in with what you were doing before, it is pretty hard to schedule their projectile vomit, teething problems and a virus that keeps them home and you away from work for days.

9. You will survive on three hours' sleep per night, relish three-minute showers, dodge urine accidents, clean up the most repulsive number twos and start going to the bathroom with an audience. Despite your worst day, you will naturally look forward to the next day and what your child's innocence, presence, laughter, personality and smiles will bring into your heart.

10. Motherhood gives you a chance to become the best person you can be if you embrace the responsibility to be the ultimate role model for this little being who thinks the world of you. As you start your new role, you have the opportunity, excuse and choice to really become the person *they* see: a beautiful, loving, generous, clever, funny woman who knows so much and can even make the booboos go away.

'Motherhood can transform you into a better version of who you thought you were ... if you are up for the challenge.'

— Christie Nicholas

THE NEW RULES

Ten rules all mums must live by

Rule #1

I will remember my needs as a woman.

Rule #2

I will enjoy and appreciate the special moments.

Rule #3

I will run away from it all occasionally to do something wonderful for me.

Rule #4

I will ask for help, advice and support.

Rule #5

I will surround myself with people who bring out my best.

Rule #6

I will not sweat the small stuff.

Rule #7

I will not compare myself or compete with other mums.

Rule #8

I will invest time, love and energy into my relationship.

Rule #9

I will always be Number 1.

Rule #10

I will be the mum who roared.

RULE #1: I WILL REMEMBER MY NEEDS AS A WOMAN

I will take time out on a regular basis to think about what I want for myself as a woman and what would make me happy, balanced and fulfilled.

RULE #2: I WILL ENJOY AND APPRECIATE THE SPECIAL MOMENTS

As much as life can get in the way of living, I know I will never get another chance at today. I will take the time daily to pause, look at my baby and remember that I am the luckiest person in the world to have this miracle staring back at me.

RULE #3: I WILL RUN AWAY FROM IT ALL OCCASIONALLY TO DO SOMETHING WONDERFUL FOR ME

I am not neglecting my child if I take some time out from being a mother. In fact, by nurturing myself and doing something that I enjoy, I am becoming a stronger, happier, healthier mum.

RULE #4: I WILL ASK FOR HELP, ADVICE AND SUPPORT

It takes a village to raise a child, so I will not expect to do it all by myself. I will ask for advice and support from others I love, trust or admire who can offer me knowledge, wisdom, help and the care I need.

RULE #5: I WILL SURROUND MYSELF WITH PEOPLE WHO BRING OUT MY BEST

I will make friends and join groups that will bring out the best in my personality, recognise my feelings, provide support and nurture my needs as a mother and a woman.

RULE #6: I WILL NOT SWEAT THE SMALL STUFF

I will not sweat the small stuff. It really doesn't matter if the beds are not made every day, if my husband bought the wrong brand of wipes and if I am late to work by eight minutes. I will save my energy and worry for the bigger things in life, and in the meantime, I will spend more time laughing, enjoying motherhood, womanhood and all the great things I am surrounded by.

RULE #7: I WILL NOT COMPARE MYSELF OR COMPETE WITH OTHER MUMS

There is no point comparing myself to other mums because everyone is different. If I try to compete or compare, I will stress myself out so it is better that I continue to concentrate on how I am raising a child as effectively, responsibly and healthily as I possibly can.

RULE #8: I WILL INVEST TIME, LOVE AND ENERGY INTO MY RELATIONSHIP

I need, want and value having my partner in my life. It is a priority that we spend quality time together enjoying each other, communicating and demonstrating the love, support and dedication we share for our relationship as man and woman.

RULE #9: I WILL ALWAYS BE NUMBER 1

Whether I am a patient mum or a frustrated mum, a working mum or a stay-at-home mum, I love my child more than anyone else possibly can and there will never be a time when someone stands before me; my child will always know who I am and what they mean to me.

RULE #10: I WILL BE THE MUM WHO ROARED

I am a mother, but I am also a woman, and I will be as sexy, smart, interesting, charismatic and brilliant as my mind tells me to be.

A–Z SUMMARY

The key points to remember

A	**ASKING FOR HELP**	1. Ask for help. 2. Accept offers of help. 3. Let go of unnecessary tasks. 4. Don't feel guilty about relying on others. 5. Those who love you will want to help.
B	**BABYMOON PERIOD**	1. After giving birth take six weeks off. 2. Use the time to nourish body and bond with baby. 3. Don't expect too much from yourself too soon. 4. Outsource as many duties as you can. 5. Listen to what your body needs.
C	**CONFIDENCE BUILDING**	1. Practise what you have learnt. 2. Trust and believe in yourself. 3. Fake it till you make it. 4. Enjoy the moment. 5. Have a positive attitude.
D	**DIET**	1. Eating well affects how you feel and function. 2. Learn about your nutritional requirements. 3. Don't set unrealistic expectations. 4. Prepare and organise your meals in advance. 5. Identify a reward to motivate you to eat well.
E	**EXERCISE**	1. See a doctor before starting an exercise regime. 2. Exercise improves your mental and physical health. 3. Exercise will assist with weight loss. 4. Start slow. 5. Make exercise a part of your lifestyle.
F	**FRIENDSHIPS**	1. Existing friendships can change. 2. Make friends with others who relate to your journey. 3. Friends provide support and encouragement. 4. Meet people via community activities and online. 5. Genuine friends brighten the good and bad days.

G	**GOAL SETTING**	1. Set goals when you feel ready to. 2. Goal setting helps you organise your life. 3. It is a way to define what you want to accomplish. 4. Goal setting provides a sense of purpose. 5. Goals should be specific, realistic and measurable.
H	**HUMOUR**	1. A sense of humour will help you overcome hurdles. 2. Others have experienced worse and survived. 3. What stresses you now will make you laugh later. 4. Choose to look at the funny side of situations. 5. Talking to others lightens the seriousness of issues.
I	**IDENTITY**	1. It is easy to neglect your needs as an individual. 2. New demands take over your life if you let them. 3. Invest the extra effort to prioritise your needs. 4. Find a passion, spend time away from daily demands, learn to juggle, and chat to others. 5. Value who you are not just what you do.
J	**JOINING A GROUP**	1. Joining a group wards off isolation. 2. Groups provide an opportunity to reconnect with society. 3. Community groups introduce you to others like you. 4. Join a group you are truly interested in. 5. Learn new things, meet others and break the routine.
K	**KEEPING UP APPEAR-ANCES**	1. Take pride in how you look and respect yourself. 2. Get out of the mum uniform, you are still a woman. 3. Adopt an improvised personal maintenance routine. 4. Make an effort for yourself, not only for your partner. 5. Be a great role model by looking after yourself.
L	**LOVE, SEX AND ROMANCE**	1. Parents can still enjoy an active and fulfilling love life. 2. A healthy love life takes extra effort but it's worth it to stay connected with your partner. 3. Feel sexy and start looking forward to sex. 4. Start new romantic habits that fit in with your new life. 5. Remember to have fun.
M	**MONEY MATTERS**	1. Understand your financial situation. 2. Set a budget. 3. Establish spending boundaries. 4. Still treat yourself, but in moderation. 5. Learn savvy savings tips.

N	**NURTURING YOURSELF**	1. Less time for yourself leaves you depleted. 2. Care for yourself in order to better care for others. 3. Listen to what your body wants. 4. Work at having balance in life, including time for you. 5. Nurture yourself with pampering, me time, treats and fewer commitments.
O	**ORGAN-ISATIONAL SKILLS**	1. Decide what you need and what you want to achieve. 2. Prioritise tasks and let go of what is non-essential. 3. Organise yourself and become more productive. 4. Gain more time, balance, calm and control. 5. Be flexible and accept that plans will change.
P	**POSITIVE THINKING**	1. Don't let circumstances dictate your mood. 2. Believe in yourself and what you are capable of. 3. Persevere after a setback. 4. Replace negative thoughts with positive thoughts. 5. Think positive to feel confident, happy and motivated.
Q	**QUESTIONS**	1. Beat boredom by keeping the mind stimulated. 2. Overcome baby blues by confiding to someone, getting help and looking forward to something. 3. Reclaim your body with healthy habits. 4. Motherhood can redefine your values for the better. 5. Participate in life to avoid loneliness.
R	**REWARDS OF MOTHERHOOD**	1. Respect and appreciate your body more than ever. 2. Live life more selflessly. 3. Redefine your priorities in life. 4. Experience unconditional love. 5. Grow closer to the extended family.
S	**SELF-ESTEEM**	1. Self-esteem is the opinion you have about yourself. 2. High self-esteem + self confidence = success. 3. Self-esteem affects your ability to realise your dreams. 4. Work on yourself and feel better about who you are. 5. Love yourself by thinking more highly of who you are.
T	**TIPS FROM OTHER MOTHERS**	1. Good time-management techniques make life easier. 2. Put your needs ahead of others. 3. Let go of the guilt. 4. Live up to your realistic expectations, not others. 5. Don't try to be perfect.

U	UNDERDOGS WHO INSPIRE	1. 2. 3. 4. 5.	Don't be daunted by challenges and setbacks. Follow your dream and pursue a passion. Have a go, even if you start with small steps. Your life is what you make of it, so live big. Accept that priorities will change.
V	VISUAL-ISATION TECHNIQUES	1. 2. 3. 4. 5.	Define what you want by visualising it. Visualise success to feel good instantly. Replay the scene of achieving a goal in your mind. If the mind can dream it, the body can achieve it. Make time to visualise daily.
W	WORKING AND THE WONDER WOMAN MYTH	1. 2. 3. 4. 5.	Working and full-time mums each have challenges. Working can make you feel better about yourself. Re-enter the workforce by updating your résumé, volunteering, contacting ex-workmates and researching companies you want to work for. Juggle life by outsourcing, cooking in bulk, saying no. Focus on being happy not perfect.
X	X-FACTOR	1. 2. 3. 4. 5.	If you feel ordinary or depleted do something about it. You deserve to feel alive, sexy, fulfilled and healthy. Work your best assets and believe in yourself. Expect the best. Make an effort to stay connected to your true self.
Y	YOU AND YOUR NEEDS	1. 2. 3. 4. 5.	Address your mental, physical and emotional needs. Be responsible for yourself. Be honest about how you feel and what you want. Address symptoms if you are often unwell and unhappy. You give the best when you have the best to offer.
Z	ZING WHEN YOU'RE ZONKED!	1. 2. 3. 4. 5.	Sleep to prevent depression, weight gain and illness. You can cope with interrupted sleep habits. Nap when baby naps, accept help, get to bed earlier. Sleep easy with less caffeine, more relaxation, and a milky drink. Re-energise with exercise, a shower, and healthy food.

GOAL CARDS

100 ways to kick start your journey

Here are 100 goal cards for you to cut out and use as inspiration. There are also ten blank goal cards for you to complete — use them to kick start your dreams!

Today I will ask someone to bring over a meal.	Today I will ask someone to help me with some housework.	Today I will ask someone to mind the baby.
Today I will ask someone to pick up some groceries for me.	Today I will ask someone for a big hug.	Today I will take the phone off the hook.
Today I will stay in my pyjamas all day.	Today I will not do any housework.	Today I will rest when the baby rests.
Today I will say no to visitors.	Today I will list five great skills I have as a mother.	Today I will get out of my comfort zone.
Today I will be kind to myself.	Today I will book a holiday.	Today I will ask someone to give me encouragement.
Today I will prepare a nutritious shopping list.	Today I will remove unhealthy foods from the kitchen.	Today I will plan five healthy meals for the week.
Today I will prepare my healthy food for the day.	Today I will start a new healthy eating habit.	Today I will find an exercise buddy.
Today I will go for a walk.	Today I will put my exercise clothes in full view.	Today I will say 'no' to extra demands on my day and energy.

Today I will get an exercise DVD.	Today I will phone my best friend.	Today I will make plans to catch up with friends.
Today I will join an online community group that addresses my needs and interests.	Today I will research community groups that I could join to make new friends.	Today I will invite someone over for coffee.
Today I will set five goals I want to achieve for the week, month, year.	Today I will start writing down my goal/s for the day.	Today I will start swapping babysitting duties with a friend.
Today I will pick one goal to focus on and take a step closer to realising it.	Today I will find a mentor.	Today I will apply for a job.
Today I will reflect on some funny experiences I have had as a mother.	Today I will brainstorm how I can make money from my strengths, experiences and abilities.	Today I will call or meet up with someone who makes me laugh.
Today I will identify my dream job and career path.	Today I will contact my ex-workmates and bosses.	Today I will do something just for me.
Today I will think about what my dream life is.	Today I will identify a passion and work out how I can spend more time doing it.	Today I will start a class or a course that interests me as a person.
Today I will write down how I want to be remembered and spoken about.	Today I will reflect on my skills.	Today I will try out a playgroup.
Today I will update my résumé.	Today I will find a friend with similar interests who wants to join a group with me.	Today I will scour the local newspaper for groups or events in which I could participate in the neighbourhood.
Today I will book a hair appointment.	Today I will book a pampering treatment.	Today I will start a new weekly at-home beauty ritual.

Today I will start a small daily habit that makes me feel beautiful.	Today I will throw out unflattering clothes.	Today I will replace old, frumpy underwear with something more beautiful.
Today I will have sex.	Today I will organise date night.	Today I will go somewhere new.
Today I will spend some quality time talking with my partner.	Today I will arrange to donate time, money or product to a charity, community group or friend in need.	Today I will review our financial situation and be clear about money coming in and money going out.
Today I will set a budget.	Today I will adopt three new savings tips as part of our lifestyle.	Today I will shower and dress first thing in the morning.
Today I will sell or swap things I no longer need.	Today I will have a bubble bath.	Today I will go out on my own.
Today I will go shopping for myself.	Today I will watch my favourite movie.	Today I will treat myself to lunch out at a restaurant.
Today I will de-clutter my home.	Today I will try a different routine.	Today I will spend fifteen minutes visualising a big, audacious dream.
Today I will delegate three tasks.	Today I will prioritise what I want to achieve.	Today I will replace any negative comments with positive ones.
Today I will write down five things I am grateful for.	Today I will think about all the wonderful things I have achieved.	Today I will smile at everyone and say hello to strangers.
Today I will go to bed 30 minutes earlier.	Today I will call my mum and let her know how much I love her.	Today I will acknowledge a setback and do something to get over it.

Today I will confide in someone about how I am really feeling.	Today I will get a make-over.	Today I will encourage and reassure my partner that he is doing a great job.
Today I will not micro-manage how my partner feeds, bathes, settles the baby.	Today I will be very nice to myself and those around me.	Today I will get a massage.
Today I will look in the mirror and say what I love about myself.	Today I will do whatever makes me happy.	Today I will tell my partner what I love about them.
Today I will lie down for fifteen minutes every time the baby naps before I do anything else.	Today I will dress up for no reason.	Today I will wear my favourite perfume for me.
Today I will resolve to improve an area of my life or myself.	Today I will stop dwelling on a negative experience and move on for good.	Today I will stop doing 'things' and just enjoy playing, laughing, cuddling and loving my baby.
Today I will believe I am the superstar my baby thinks I am.	Today I will	Today I will
Today I will	Today I will	Today I will
Today I will	Today I will	Today I will
Today I will	Today I will	

INDEX